Seven Great Principles

2nd Edition

Dag Heward-Mills

Parchment House

Unless otherwise stated, all Scripture quotations are taken from the King James Version of the Bible.

Copyright © 2000, 2018 Dag Heward-Mills

SEVEN GREAT PRINCIPLES - 2ND EDITION

First Edition published by Parchment House, 2000
ISBN: 9988-596-12-X

Second Edition Published by Parchment House, 2019
1st Printing 2019

Find out more about Dag Heward-Mills at:

Healing Jesus Campaign
Email: evangelist@daghewardmills.org
Website: www.daghewardmills.org
Facebook: Dag Heward-Mills
Twitter: @EvangelistDag

ISBN: 978-1-64329-196-3

Contents

Chapter 1

Principles

Wisdom is the principal thing; therefore get wisdom: and with all thy getting get understanding. Exalt her, and she shall promote thee: she shall bring thee to honour, when thou dost embrace her. She shall give to thine head an ornament of grace: a crown of glory shall she deliver to thee.

Proverbs 4:7-9

This book contains a collection of principles. A principle is a revelation! A principle is a deep understanding of how something works. All the principles in this book relate to the great salvation that we have experienced in Christ. A principle is something that allows you to develop!

It was a principle that allowed human beings to develop the bicycle, the wheelbarrow and then the car. It is principles that allowed human beings to develop trucks, tractors, trams and then trains.

It was principles that allowed human beings to fly kites, then aeroplanes and now rockets. It was principles that allowed men to create a bow and arrow, then a pistol, then a machine gun, missiles and then inter-continental ballistic missiles. A principle just allows you to go further and deeper.

Each of these vehicles operates on the same principles. Once you get the principle right, you can do many other things.

Learn great principles because they are great foundations upon which you can develop.

If you are not tired of learning you will not be tired of rising! These principles are going to place in your hand, keys that will ensure your rising into higher levels in God.

Salvation is a major surgery that has taken place in your soul. Salvation can be likened to a heart transplant! God has taken out the stony heart and replaced it with a heart of flesh! If you are born again, you have had a spiritual heart transplant. This book is to help you understand what has happened to you. After surgery, the doctors have to sit down with you and explain what they did to you. The doctors have to tell you the implications of the surgery that they have performed.

This book is to help you to have a deeper understanding of the concept of salvation. Through these seven great principles, God will give you a new understanding that will make you grow in grace.

Wisdom is the principal thing! Get understanding! You need wisdom and you need understanding if you are to do well in Christ. You gain understanding when you know principles.

Many Christians are confused about their salvation. They think they have just joined another religion. Christianity is much more than a religion! Christianity is the experience of a great change in your life.

People with understanding are those who will experience God's victory. I see you blessed as you understand these seven great principles! I see you enjoying your salvation! I see you growing in this great salvation! I see you becoming established in Christ!

Chapter 2

Seven Great Principles of Salvation

How shall we escape, if we neglect so GREAT SALVATION; which at the first began to be spoken by the Lord, and was confirmed unto us by them that heard him;

Hebrews 2:3

PRINCIPLE No. 1

MAN IS A SPIRIT, HAS A SOUL AND LIVES IN A BODY

And the very God of peace sanctify you wholly; and I pray God your whole SPIRIT and SOUL and BODY be preserved blameless unto the coming of our Lord Jesus Christ.

1 Thessalonians 5:23

The fact that a human being is actually a spirit living inside a physical body is one of the lesser known truths. When Paul wrote to the Thessalonians he wrote that God should affect them in all three areas: spirit, soul and body.

A human being is not just a piece of meat. When Princess Diana died many people in this world reflected on the reality of spiritual issues. I spoke to somebody in the lobby of Novotel Accra. He asked me what I did and I told him that I was a pastor. "Oh, I see," he said.

"Do you believe in God?" I asked him.

"Actually, I had just been thinking about this."

He continued, "When Princess Diana died I wondered whether I was just a piece of meat."

I told him, "You are not just a piece of meat. There is more to you than a piece of meat."

When people speak in a very proud and arrogant way, it is because they are not aware of how real eternal things are.

Is there more to this life?

I will never forget my first day as a medical student in one of the laboratories at the University of Ghana Medical School. It was about 2 o'clock in the afternoon when we were ushered into a large air-conditioned room containing twelve white marble tables. On each of these tables was a dead human being lying stark naked. There were about ten dead men and two dead women. My friends and I gathered around one of the tables. There were stools around each table and I sat down staring at the dead body that lay before me. On the chest of this human being was a plaster with a name inscribed on it. The name of our cadaver was Cornelius. I wondered to myself, "Who was Cornelius during his lifetime? What did he do for a living? How did he come to lie before us, ready for eighteen months of intensive dissection?"

As we sat there, our Anatomy lecturer came in. He happened to be a Christian. He said to us, "Go ahead and touch them, don't be afraid!" But in spite of his encouragement, most people were scared by the whole scene.

This Anatomy lecturer said something that has stayed with me since then. He said, "This scene should make everyone of you seriously consider what life is all about." He added, "If life just consists of the physical then even goats are better. Because when goats die they can be eaten, but human beings cannot be eaten."

I thought about that statement and I realized that life must consist of more than what we see physically. *Man is a spirit.* The Bible says that God is the Father of spirits.

> **...shall we not much rather be in subjection unto the FATHER OF SPIRITS, and live?**
>
> **Hebrews 12:9**

If God is the Father of spirits, then we His children are spirits. That means that our bodies are just containers of the spirit. The Bible describes the body as a house.

> **For we know that if our EARTHLY HOUSE of this tabernacle were dissolved, we have a building of God, an house not made with hands, eternal in the heavens.**
>
> **2 Corinthians 5:1**

When Lazarus of Luke 16 died, the Bible teaches us that he was carried by the angels into Abraham's bosom.

And it came to pass, that the beggar died, and was carried by the angels into Abraham's bosom...

Luke 16:22

I once passed by an unmarked grave. I saw three men throwing dead bodies into the mass grave. I went up to the car and asked, "What are you doing?" They were hospital officials who had been sent to bury unclaimed bodies. I immediately remembered Lazarus. These were modern-day Lazaruses. But that is not the end of the story. After the body dies, the spirit lives on!

Lazarus himself, the real man, was carried into Abraham's bosom. Remember also the testimony of the rich man. He had everything in life. He had better health care so he lived longer than Lazarus. However, it came to pass that he also died. He probably had a grand funeral.

Where Did They Go?

Years ago, I attended a funeral of someone. His funeral was very grand. Dignitaries travelled from all over the country to attend the funeral. Special invitation cards were issued for the funeral. The corpse had several changes of clothing during the night. The most amazing part of the funeral was that a new road was actually constructed in the town to enable everybody to attend the funeral in comfort.

I don't know if you are aware of the cost of constructing a road. No expenses were spared for the funeral of this great rich man. This funeral also reminded me of the story of the rich man in the book of Luke. But the story does not end there.

He Went to Hell

The Bible says in Hell he lifted up his eyes. The man still had eyes even though he was in Hell. He cried out to Father Abraham that he should allow Lazarus to dip the tip of his finger in water to cool his tongue.

> **And in hell he lift up his EYES, being in torments, and SEETH Abraham afar off, and Lazarus in his bosom. And he CRIED [mouth/voice] and said, Father Abraham, have mercy on me, and send Lazarus, that he may dip the tip of his FINGER in water and cool my TONGUE; for I am tormented in this flame.**
>
> **Luke 16:23,24**

Notice that different parts of the body have been mentioned. The picture of a man is being painted. This is interesting because the Bible describes the spirit of a man as the hidden man, the inward man or the inner man.

Dear friend, the Lazarus who was in Abraham's bosom was the real Lazarus. It was the soul and spirit of Lazarus. The rich man who was languishing in Hell was not the rich man who had been buried at that lavish funeral. It was the soul and the spirit of the rich man that was experiencing the fires of Hell. You can verify for yourself, whether the body stays in the grave or not! The mortal remains of human beings remain on earth long after the spirit has departed to eternal life or damnation.

I know that many Christians are not aware of this great reality: that they are spirit, soul and body. When many Christians wake up in the morning, they spend a long time bathing, brushing their teeth and getting ready.

You are More Than a Body

Many ladies spend a long time getting ready to go out. After that they may have a good breakfast or lunch before moving out. Then these born-again Christians walk out of the door without even saying a five-minute prayer. This is because they are not aware that they are more than a body. It is only because they are not conscious that they are spirits living in a body that they spend all their time on the body only.

When a person becomes aware of his spirit and soul, he spends time to build up and develop the spirit.

Many governments are not aware that a human being is made up of more than just a body and a mind. They stress education and physical fitness but they leave out the real person. Man is a spiritual being first of all. The mind and the body are just mortal containers of the human spirit.

Develop the Human Spirit

It is time for Christians to be aware of the spirit that dwells in them. It is time for us to develop the human spirit. You can develop your human spirit by praying.

He that speaketh in an unknown tongue EDIFIETH [builds up, charges] HIMSELF...

1 Corinthians 14:4

The Bible says that when you speak in tongues you build up, charge and edify your spirit. It is good to do bodily exercises. We are not against that! But what about spiritual exercises? Be conscious of your spirit within. You are a spirit, you have a soul and you live in a body.

But what is a soul? The Bible makes it clear that the soul is different from the spirit.

For the word of God is quick, and powerful, and sharper than any twoedged sword, piercing even to the dividing asunder of SOUL and SPIRIT...

Hebrews 4:12

There is a dividing asunder (a demarcation) between the spirit and the soul of a man. There are so many words in the Bible that are used to describe the actions of the soul. The soul can be said to be rejoicing (Psalms 31:7). The soul can magnify and bless the Lord (Psalms 103:2). The soul can be downcast (Psalms 42:5). The soul can be grieved (Judges 10:16). The soul can be discouraged (Numbers 21:4). The soul can be joyful (Psalms 35:9).

These are just a few of the emotions that the soul expresses. We can therefore conclude that the soul is the part of the man that experiences thoughts, feelings and emotions.

The Soul Lives On

You will realize that the soul of the rich man was alive in Hell. That is why he could remember Lazarus. The rich man thought things were still the same as when he was alive on earth. That is why he wanted to send Lazarus like a messenger, to come all the way from Heaven to Hell to serve him some water.

The rich man remembered his five brothers and pleaded with Father Abraham to prevent them from coming to join him in Hell. He pitied anyone who would ever come to Hell. The soul of the rich man had perished in the lake of fire and he could remember, think and feel as though he was on earth.

What did Jesus say about the soul? He said, "What shall it profit a man if he shall gain the whole world and lose his soul?" It is the soul that goes to Hell. Your spirit and your soul will suffer in Hell.

For what shall it profit a man, if he shall gain the whole world, and LOSE HIS OWN SOUL?

Mark 8:36

PRINCIPLE No. 2

THE SPIRIT OF AN UNSAVED MAN IS DEAD AND DESPERATELY WICKED

The heart [unsaved spirit] is DECEITFUL above all things, and DESPERATELY WICKED: who can know it?

Jeremiah 17:9

When a person is not born-again he has what I call an unsaved spirit. There are many different ways the Bible describes an unbeliever. The Bible calls a non-Christian an unbeliever, a sinner and unregenerate. It is important for you to be aware of the condition of the human spirit.

The Word of God makes it abundantly clear that anyone who is not a believer has an unregenerate spirit and is capable of many evil things. The fact that an unsaved man is in a terrible spiritual condition is made abundantly clear in Romans chapter one. The Bible says that God's wrath is being released against the wickedness of men.

> **For the wrath of God is revealed from heaven against all ungodliness and unrighteousness of men...**
>
> **Romans 1:18**

The human race has forsaken the living God and therefore God has given them up to become dead and darkened in their spirits.

> **Because that when they knew God, they glorified him not as God, neither were thankful; become vain in their imaginations, AND THEIR FOOLISH HEART WAS DARKENED.**
>
> **Romans 1:21**

The heart of the unsaved person is darkened and degenerate. God has gone a step further and given up on mankind so that they may follow their own desires and perverted feelings.

> **Wherefore GOD ALSO GAVE THEM UP TO UNCLEANNESS through the lusts of their own hearts, to dishonour their own bodies between themselves:**
>
> **Romans 1:24**

Not only is the spirit of the unsaved man darkened with death but the mind of the unsaved human race has also degenerated into a depraved condition.

And even as they did not like to retain God in their knowledge, GOD GAVE THEM OVER TO A REPROBATE MIND to do those things which are not convenient;

Romans 1:28

As you read this passage further, you will discover that the sinful human race is filled with every conceivable evil. The long list of evil characteristics is there for your reading.

Being filled with all unrighteousness, fornication, wickedness, covetousness maliciousness; full of envy, murder, debate, deceit, malignity; whisperers, Backbiters, haters of God, despiteful, proud, boasters, inventors of evil things, disobedient to parents, Without understanding, covenantbreakers, without natural affection, implacable, unmerciful:

Romans 1:29-31

This principle that an unsaved spirit is desperately wicked is manifest every day of our lives. God has warned Christians against marrying non-Christians because a non-Christian has an unregenerate spirit and is capable of many evil things. One of the things that an unbeliever is filled with is covenant breaking (Romans 1:31). Most unbelievers do not stick to their word. It is rare to find an unbeliever who is faithful to his marriage covenant. One man told me, "I have never seen a faithful unbeliever husband before."

As I grew up in life I came to discover that covenant breaking was part and parcel of the unbeliever's lifestyle. They say, "I will" and "I do", but they won't and they don't. This is the reason why God says Christians should not marry unbelievers. Do not think that God is trying to punish you by telling you not to marry an unbeliever. God is trying to prevent your heart from being broken by a covenant breaker.

Do not be deceived by the dignified appearance of the unbeliever. He may be a school prefect, a class prefect, a minister of state or even the president. The nature of an unsaved person is described in detail for you in Romans 1:29-31. Believe in the Bible more than you believe your eyes. The Bible is the Word of God and is profitable for your instruction. (2 Timothy 3:16)

No one teaches a child to be wicked. Wickedness comes naturally to many little children. Why do children lie, cheat and steal without being taught to do so? It is because the unsaved sprit is at work again.

When I was in secondary school, I couldn't understand the manifestation of wickedness in some of the students. They devised all sorts of unbelievable punishments. When I was in form one, I experienced torture at the hands of senior students. These senior students were not torture specialists. They were just seniors with an unsaved nature.

They could mash chloroquine tablets (a bitter anti-malarial drug) in gari (ground grilled cassava granules) and give it to people to eat. They had punishments called "tower of liberty" and "monkey dance" which would make all your muscles go into spasms. I was once forced to do a "monkey dance" until I was virtually paralyzed. I couldn't walk for hours.

Punishments were devised in which you would be sent to collect twenty buckets of manure from a farm two kilometres away. After doing this twenty times, you would have walked eighty kilometres with a heavy load.

Where did all these ideas come from? They originate from the depraved and wicked heart of the unsaved man. I ask myself, "If such people were to come into political power what would they do to their enemies?"

All over the world, the depraved and perverted nature of the human race is manifest. When I hear of the atrocities committed during wars I wonder, "What has become of the human race?" Wickedness abounds in the heart of man because the heart of the unsaved man is dead and desperately wicked. This is not something that affects White people or Black people; it is the nature of all mankind.

During the Liberian Civil War we heard of people being fed to lions. One Liberian refugee told me how the rebel soldiers would throw children into a well. When the well was full of children they would pour kerosene on top of the screaming children and light a fire. These are real things that actually happened!

Why are human beings so wicked and evil at heart? Why is it that when the opportunity presents itself we see incredible acts of savagery?

A Lebanese man described something that he experienced during the war in Lebanon. He said, "One group would capture some prisoners that belonged to another faction. Then they would amputate the legs and arms of the captives and put the trunk (head, chest and abdomen, without legs and arms) of the people in a car and dispatch them to their homes." He told me how a friend's brother's arms and legs were amputated and how terrible an experience it was. He continued, "The limbless man was in such a pitiful condition that my friend had to shoot his own brother to end his suffering."

These acts of barbarism are manifestations of a depraved and reprobate human race. Why is the world filled with so much evil? Why do millions of people commit fornication and adultery on a daily basis? Why does stealing, killing and injustice abound everywhere? Where is this world of over five billion greedy, corrupt, degenerate and selfish people going?

God has given up the human race to its perverted way of life. It is these unsaved and degenerate people that Jesus came to the earth to save. This is why Jesus said a man had to be born-again. Another term for being born-again is regeneration. When you are born-again, your essential nature is changed. That is why the Bible calls you a new creature. God has to make a new creation out of the old corrupt man.

When a man dies, there is no way you can keep his body at home. No matter how much you love your brother, when the condition called death lays its icy hands on him you have to part company with him. The dead person must go to the mortuary and then the grave. Husbands and wives who love each other have to part when death comes to lay hold on one of them. Why is this? The body of your loved one is dead. It begins to decay and degenerate.

Do you remember what God told Adam and Eve? He said that, "In the day that you eat this fruit you will die." When Adam and Eve sinned, they died. The condition of spiritual death entered their spirits and there was no way God could fellowship with them any more. He had to drag them out of the garden and separate them from Himself. The whole human race is separate from God. Salvation breaks the wall that separates mankind from God.

> **...and hath broken down the middle wall of partition between us... that he might reconcile both unto God...**
> **Ephesians 2:14,16**

Before a man is born-again, he is estranged from God. His nature is essentially evil. He may look good on the outside, but essentially, he has a corrupt and wicked nature. That is why democracy and the rule of law are important. When one man with such a nature has unlimited power, he does many evil things.

In every nation where there has been a military dictator, inconceivable atrocities have taken place. People are arrested and disappear into "thin air", whilst hard-earned properties are arbitrarily confiscated. Stories of torture, brutality and murder abound. Viciousness in secret and in the open, has always been the order of the day with tyrants.

A tyrant is simply an unsaved man who has unlimited power. That is why many governments have three independent arms: the executive, the legislature and the judiciary. There needs to be a separation of powers because of the wickedness of mankind.

As Lord Acton (1834-1902) said in a letter to Bishop Mandell Creighton, "Power tends to corrupt and absolute power corrupts absolutely."

The difference between Christianity and every other religion is simple.

The New Creation

Christianity claims to change the essentially wicked nature of a man. Jesus makes you a new creation. You become a brand new creature with a brand new heart. In the Old Testament, the prophets predicted that the day would come when God would take out the stony heart and replace it with a heart of flesh.

A new heart also I will give you, and a new spirit will I put within you: and I will take away the stony heart out of your flesh, and I will give you an HEART OF FLESH.

Ezekiel 36:26

When a man is in Christ he is a new person. He is regenerated. He is born again. When we speak of being born-again, it does not mean going into your mother's womb again. It is your spirit, the inner nature that is born again.

...that which is born of the Spirit is spirit.

John 3:6

If you take a pig and you wash him, bathe him and dress him up in a wedding suit, all you have is a dressed up pig. This same pig will return to the filth that he is used to because that is his essential nature. Obeying a set of rules does not change your heart. Coming to Christ and being born-again is what affords every man the opportunity to have a new heart.

I believe with all my heart that it is only a change in the unsaved nature of a man that can bring about a change in this world. New Year's resolutions and obeying rules do not change anything because the spirit of the unsaved man is dead and desperately wicked. No one toys with a dead thing. Dead things must be separated from living things. The only hope for the dead and wicked human spirit is the miracle of rebirth in Jesus Christ.

PRINCIPLE No. 3

THE SPIRIT OF A SAVED MAN IS RIGHTEOUS AND TRULY HOLY

And that ye put on the new man, which after God is created in RIGHTEOUSNESS AND TRUE HOLINESS.

Ephesians 4:24

When a man is born-again the spirit within is changed. We have learned earlier that the unsaved spirit is desperately wicked and corrupt. What about the new creation? The new creation is righteous and truly holy!

This Scripture makes us know that we are actually righteous when we are born-again. What God is telling us is that we must put on (act like) the new spirit which is created in righteousness and true holiness. Many times we come to God and say things that are not true. In an attempt to sound humble, we tell the Lord that we are sinners and we are not worthy to approach His throne. It is time for you to acknowledge what God has done to your heart. The Bible says we are the righteousness of God in Christ Jesus.

For he hath made him to be sin for us, who knew no sin; that we might be made the righteousness of God in him.

2 Corinthians 5:21

If we are the righteousness of God, it means that we cannot be more righteous than we are today. The righteousness of God is the highest form of purity and "sinless-ness". God is describing the status of your new spirit.

Somebody once said, "I don't feel any different now that I'm born-again!" This is not about feelings but about realities that have taken place. Can you feel your liver or your small intestines? Obviously not! But they exist within you!

If surgery was performed and your appendix was taken out, the doctors would inform you that they have removed a part of your intestine. You are supposed to accept the fact of what has taken place in your abdomen during the surgery.

Being born again is a spiritual operation in which God recreates your spirit. He takes out the old hardened and depraved heart and puts in a new and righteous spirit.

The Bible teaches us to acknowledge the good things that are in us because we are Christians. We are not supposed to go around saying negative things about ourselves. If you say, "I am a bad person," you are hurting yourself. If you say, "I'm stupid!" or "I am a sinner" you are saying something that is contrary to the Word of God. It is time to acknowledge good things about yourself.

...by the acknowledging of every good thing which is in you in Christ Jesus.

Philemon 6

Acknowledging good things will make your faith come alive. Say to yourself, "I am the righteousness of God! I'm a new person! I can make it! I am holy!" These confessions will take you out of sin and into a life of practical holiness. There is always something on the inside that must work on the outside. Righteousness on the inside is working on the outside.

Any born-again Christian who lives in sin, is living contrary to his new nature. If you continue in sin it is by choice because the power of sin is broken and God has given you a new nature. When you are a new creature it is no longer natural to do evil. It is against your very nature as a new creation.

Before you get born again there are evil things you do without even noticing. After you're saved, something within you tells you, "This is wrong! Don't do it!" That is the new man crying from within. The Bible says, "Put on the new man." Act like a new person because you are new.

I became a medical doctor on the 10th of March 1989. On the 11th of March I didn't feel any different; in fact, I still felt like a student. I had to tell myself, "Hey, you are now a doctor. Act like one. Stop acting like a student and act like who you really are." This is what God is saying to His "new creation" children, "You are new, righteous and truly holy. Act like it and walk in the newness of life."

Remember this, righteousness is not a feeling. You do not work to gain righteousness. It is impossible to attain God's standards by your own efforts. Today, if you are born-again, you have been instantaneously transformed into a righteous new man. You cannot be more righteous than the righteousness of God.

You can only increase your faith in your inherited righteousness. You can only practise more and more of your true nature. When you are conscious of your righteousness in Christ, you will become as bold as a lion.

The wicked flee when no man pursueth: but the RIGHTEOUS ARE BOLD AS A LION.

Proverbs 28:1

Through righteousness you will rule and dominate in this life. I see you dominating the enemy through righteousness! I see you overcoming your adversities through the gift of righteousness in Christ Jesus! Stand up now and become a world overcomer! You are no longer under condemnation.

...much more they which receive abundance of grace and the GIFT OF RIGHTEOUSNESS SHALL REIGN in life...

Romans 5:17

PRINCIPLE No. 4

AFTER YOU ARE BORN-AGAIN, YOUR SPIRIT IS A NEW BORN BABY AND IT MUST GROW

As newborn babes, desire the sincere milk of the word, THAT YE MAY GROW thereby:

1 Peter 2:2

When you get saved, something great has happened. There is no doubt about this. However, we must understand exactly what has happened. When somebody is born into this world, he starts life as a baby. It is important that he matures into an adult.

There are times when people have the wrong impression about Christianity. The evangelist preaches and says, "Tonight is your night! Your life will never be the same again after today." He goes on to add, "After tonight, every yoke shall be broken in your life." He declares, "All you who are heavy laden must come to Jesus and He will give you rest." This may give the impression that you instantaneously become a mature Christian.

But that is not the case at all! Being born again is just the beginning of a long process. Being born again is like being born into this world. You must go through three important stages of development. Every Christian goes through these three stages whether he knows it or not! The baby stage, the childhood stage and then the mature adult stage.

PRINCIPLE No. 5

AFTER YOU ARE SAVED, YOUR MIND IS STILL THE SAME; IT MUST BE RENEWED

And be not conformed to this world: but be ye transformed by the RENEWING OF YOUR MIND,

that ye may prove what is that good, and acceptable, and perfect, will of God.

Romans 12:2

When you are born again, God gives you a new heart but not a new mind. It is therefore the duty of every Christian to renew his mind. If you do not renew your mind, you will be a person with a new spirit and an old mind. There are many Christians who are genuine new creations but still have unrenewed minds.

If you belong to a good church which constantly preaches and teaches the Word of God, your mind will be renewed. Unfortunately, there are some people who think they know all there is to know in the Word of God.

Do not be tired of learning! Every Christian must decide to be a constant learner of the Word of God. You must never stop learning. You will always discover things that you do not know.

Years ago I heard a pastor giving a testimony of his life. Before he was saved, he was a pornographer by profession. He acted in pornographic films and posed for pornographic photographs. Sex was his work and he didn't see anything wrong with it.

He felt he was being loving each time he slept with a girl. He continued his lifestyle of fornication after he got born again, sleeping with one girl after the other. It never occurred to him that there was something wrong with sleeping with someone you were not married to.

One night, he was in bed with one of the girls when suddenly, a huge black figure appeared at the foot of his bed. He was terrified and thought to himself, "Something is not right!" The next day, he searched his Bible and discovered where the Word of God says fornication is wrong.

But fornication, and all uncleaness... let it not be once named among you, as becometh saints;

Ephesians 5:3

Believe it or not, this man was born again but because of his background, he did not even know that fornication was a sin. It could be that because of your background you are not even aware that certain things are sin.

I know some Christians who are prejudiced or even racist. There are pastors who are racist in their thoughts and decisions. Without even realizing it, we carry on doing wrong things although we are genuinely born again in our hearts. That is why we need the Word of God to renew our minds.

...be ye transformed by the RENEWING OF YOUR MIND...

Romans 12:2

It is actually the renewing of our minds that brings about a visible transformation. If you read the Bible, your mind will be renewed and your attitude will change. The real change we look for in Christians comes through a renewal of the mind in the Word of God. There are many Christians who do not tithe simply because their minds are polluted with wrong ideas. Some think the pastors are just using the money for their extravagant lifestyles. However, every Christian who has his mind renewed will find himself being transformed in the area of his finances.

How to Renew Your Mind

See your mind as a computer which has to be programmed. Whatever you feed into the mind is what will come out. Your mind will be renewed by receiving the Word. The old thoughts and ideas will be cleared out as you receive the Word.

Now ye are clean through the WORD which I have spoken unto you.

John 15:3

Your mind is also renewed by joining the right church and learning the right things. As you receive the Word through your pastor, you will gradually experience a change in your mind.

That he might sanctify and cleanse it with the washing of water by the WORD.

Ephesians 5:26

It is the renewed mind that will make you live out the new life. When people see the new life, they will know that something real has happened to you!

PRINCIPLE No. 6

AFTER YOU ARE SAVED, YOUR BODY IS STILL THE SAME; YOU MUST KEEP IT UNDER CONTROL

But I keep under my body, and bring it into subjection...

1 Corinthians 9:27

When you get saved, your body is the same old body. You do not change physically. If you were tall and skinny before salvation, you will be tall and skinny after salvation. If you had long hair before you got born again, you'll still have long hair after salvation. Does this mean that nothing has happened to you? Not at all! Your spirit is recreated in God.

When people give their lives to Christ, they often believe that everything would be different from that moment onwards. However, they get home only to realize they still have the old feelings they had before salvation. They experience lust within their bodies. The old feelings of jealousy, hatred and anger return.

The devil begins to tell them, "You are not a real Christian. You are not saved. You are not born again!" Satan continues to harass you and says, "If you were really born again, such a thought or feeling would never occur to you. Satan tells you; None of the Christians sitting in this church has the kind of thoughts you have."

But satan is a liar! We all have thoughts and feelings that we don't want to have even though we are born again. Everyone who is born again still has to contend with the flesh. Even Paul was worried about his flesh. He knew that his flesh could disgrace him one day. That is why he kept his flesh under constant control.

> **...I KEEP UNDER [control] MY BODY, and bring it into subjection: lest that by any means, when I have preached to others, I myself should be a castaway.**
>
> **1 Corinthians 9:27**

Paul had so many visions and revelations of Jesus Christ. Paul was one of the greatest apostles, with signs and wonders in his ministry. He raised the dead, and snake bites had no effect on him. Paul wrote half of the New Testament. Yet, this great man was worried about his flesh. Even though he was born again, his flesh (body) was still the same. He declared that there was nothing good in his flesh.

> **For I know that in me (that is, in my flesh,) dwelleth no good thing:...**
>
> **Romans 7:18**

No matter who you are, you still have a body to keep under control. Have you ever seen a spirit smoking, drinking, alcohol, taking drugs or watching pornography? Certainly not! It is the flesh that drinks and smokes. Have you ever seen a spirit committing fornication? Surely not! It is the flesh that does all these evil things! The works of the flesh are listed below:

> **Now the works of the flesh are manifest, which are these; Adultery, fornication, uncleanness, lasciviousness, Idolatry, witchcraft, hatred, variance, emulations, wrath, strife, seditions, heresies, envyings, murders, drunkenness, revellings, and such like:...**
>
> **Galatians 5:19-21**

These works are not the works of Satan or the works of evil spirits. Mind you, these are not just the works of the unbeliever's flesh. Do you have flesh? Of course you do! You have a body and so do I. That means that we are capable of this list of horrible deeds. The flesh is a real burden that we are saddled with throughout this life. That is why we have no confidence in the flesh.

...and have no confidence in the flesh.

Philippians 3:3

That is why we must be merciful to Christians who fall into sin, because when we consider our own selves, we realize that we experience similar temptations and feelings in our flesh.

Brethren, if a man be overtaken in a fault, ye which are spiritual, restore such an one in the spirit of meekness; considering thyself, lest thou also be tempted.

Galatians 6:1

One day when Jesus comes, our bodies shall be transformed into immortal and incorruptible bodies. We will no longer be capable of sin.

...We shall not all sleep, but we shall all be changed... for the trumpet shall sound, and the dead shall be raised incorruptible, and we shall be changed. For this corruptible must put on incorruption, and this mortal must put on immortality.

1 Corinthians 15:51-53

One day, I visited a friend of mine; a hardened sinner who was not interested in being born again. The Holy Spirit led me to witness to him about Christ. For the first time, he listened. When I finished, he asked me, "What must I do?" I led him in the sinner's prayer, and he said afterwards, "Dag, thank you very much. I feel I am a changed person." Then I decided to lead him to receive the baptism of the Holy Spirit. I laid hands on him and to my surprise, he received the Holy Spirit, speaking in tongues fluently. Suddenly something else happened. When I touched him, he was "slain in the Spirit" and fell on his bed. He spoke in tongues for some time. An hour later, I decided to leave.

Approximately five hours later, I returned to his apartment to see him. When I got there, I paused at the door before going in. What did I hear? My new convert was fornicating in the bedroom with his girlfriend! Oh dear! So soon after a wonderful salvation experience and the Holy Ghost baptism! I was aghast! I asked myself, "Was this man really born again? Does being born again have any effect on a person?"

The answer is: "Yes, it does!" The reality was that my friend's body was still the same and capable of committing all the sins of the flesh. As a baby Christian, he had yielded his flesh to all the old sins. His flesh had once more engaged itself in sin, because it had not been affected by the "born-again experience". Though you are born again, your flesh is still the same. Never forget this! Keep it under control, or else it will lead you into sin.

Control Your Flesh

There are practical ways by which you can keep your body under control. Firstly, be aware of the potential for evil that is in your flesh. Spend time fasting on a regular basis. Do not give opportunities to your flesh. What we need is wisdom to help us stay far away from dangerous enticements of the flesh.

...only use not liberty for an occasion to the flesh...

Galatians 5:13

If you expose yourself to certain things, you will fall. If I expose myself to certain things, I will fall. God said very clearly, "Flee youthful lusts." If God knew we could win the fight for fleshly control, he would have told us to fight. When God says run, then you must run! Don't stand and fight. Flee for your life! Your body is still the same. Don't trust yourself to your flesh; there is no good thing in your body. Give no place to the devil and give no opportunity to your flesh!

Neither give place to the devil.

Ephesians 4:27

PRINCIPLE No. 7

AFTER YOU ARE BORN AGAIN, YOUR MIND IS STILL OPEN TO ALL KINDS OF THOUGHTS; YOU MUST LEARN TO THINK ON THE RIGHT THINGS

Casting down imaginations, and every high thing that exalteth itself against the knowledge of God, and bringing into captivity every thought to the obedience of Christ;

2 Corinthians 10:5

You may be a born-again Christian who keeps his body under subjection, and renews your mind on the Word of God regularly, but your mind is still open to all kinds of thoughts from the devil. The devil will always appeal to your mind. The Bible teaches us that we must cast down imaginations.

Your mind is the battleground. Satan's most powerful tool is "suggestion". He tempted Jesus through the avenue of His thoughts.

A thought is like a bird that flies over your head. It may land on your head, but it must not be allowed to make a nest on your head. When ungodly thoughts come to you, resist them immediately. Do not be surprised when outrageous things occur to you. That is the fight of every born-again Christian; to keep your mind pure at all times.

The devil plagues us with thoughts of fear and worry. When I was a medical student, I saw many young patients die on the hospital ward. Soon, a spirit of fear oppressed me. I imagined myself dying of the same diseases, and I even worked out every detail of my funeral in my mind. Fear is an oppressive spirit that works through the mind. I had to shake off the fears and anxieties that were invading my soul.

Whether it is worry, fear, or lust, you must learn to cast down wrong imaginations. Capture your thoughts and make them obedient to the Word of God. Resist the devil by resisting the thoughts and suggestions that come from the pit of Hell.

Finally, brethren, whatsoever things are true, whatsoever things are honest, whatsoever things are just, whatsoever things are pure, whatsoever things are lovely, whatsoever things are of good report; if there be any virtue, and if there be any praise, think on these things.

Philippians 4:8

The Bible tells us exactly what to think about. It tells us to think of things that are pure, holy and peaceful.

Control Your Thoughts

One of the best ways to control your thoughts is to listen to preaching tapes. Christian music and videos are good tools to help in controlling your thoughts. Do not give place to the devil. You give place to the devil when you allow evil thoughts to settle in your mind. They will oppress and obsess you until you become possessed.

Chapter 3

Seven Great Principles for a Great Change

But they had heard only, That HE WHICH PERSECUTED US IN TIMES PAST NOW PREACHETH the faith which once he destroyed.

Galatians 1:23

Many people claim to be born again but there is no great change in their lives. After you are saved, you must fight to experience a great change in your life. What is the point of salvation if there is no great change in you? How can you be as lazy as you were before, as immoral as you were before, or as quarrelsome as you were before? Salvation is supposed to bring about a great change in you.

When I got born again, my mother commented to one of her friends. She said; I don't know and I don't understand what it means to be born again but one thing I know is that my son has changed. You see, people who don't go to church must be able to see a great change in you. People who don't understand Christianity must be able to see that a great change has come over you. Most unbelievers will never read the Bible. However, most unbelievers, who will never read the Bible, will meet you. They will interact with you. You will be the message of salvation to them. Your changed life will be the testimony they need to see. The great change in your life will speak to them. They will look at the change in your life and be inspired.

In this chapter, we want to study how a great change will come about in your life after you are born again. The fact that there is no change in your life since you got saved does not mean that your salvation is not real. Salvation is very real. Jesus changes lives. If your life is not changed, it is because there are certain things you are not doing properly. These are the seven principles that will ensure that a great change takes place in your life.

PRINCIPLE No. 1

AFTER YOU ARE BORN AGAIN, A GREAT CHANGE WILL COME INTO YOUR LIFE IF YOU GROW UP SPIRITUALLY

And I, brethren, could not speak unto you as unto spiritual, but as unto carnal, even as unto BABES IN CHRIST. I have fed you with milk, and not with meat:

**for hitherto ye were not able to bear it, neither yet now
are ye able.**

1 Corinthians 3:1-2

Man is made up of a spirit, a soul (mind) and a body. After
you are born again, your spirit is a new-born baby. You have
a new heart. As you know, the heart or the spirit of man is the
seat of all our human behaviour. When the heart of a man is
changed, his behaviour changes. The heart of a man is his spirit.
If your spirit is a tiny little undeveloped baby, it will not be able
to influence your mind and your body.

What influence does a baby have on society? Very little! But
if a baby grows up, it can have a great influence on society. All
men who have influenced this world were once tiny little babies
carried by their mothers. Allow your spirit to grow into a "man"
by feeding on the word of God! Allow your spirit to grow by
speaking in tongues! Allow your spirit to grow by fellowshipping
regularly in the house of God! If your spirit is developed, it will
influence your mind and your body. Your developed grown-up
spirit will begin to show great changes in your life.

PRINCIPLE No. 2

AFTER YOU ARE BORN AGAIN, A GREAT CHANGE WILL COME IN YOUR LIFE IF YOU RENEW YOUR MIND WITH THE WORD OF GOD

**I beseech you therefore, brethren, by the mercies of
God, that ye present your bodies a living sacrifice,
holy, acceptable unto God, which is your reasonable
service. And be not conformed to this world: BUT
BE YE TRANSFORMED BY THE RENEWING OF
YOUR MIND, that ye may prove what is that good,
and acceptable, and perfect, will of God.**

Romans 12:1-2

Transformation takes place because of the renewing or reprograming of your mind. Without the renewing of the mind, there will be no transformation and no change!

Since you have found Jesus, everybody is waiting for the great change in your life. Salvation is always accompanied by a great change. Yet, many people do not show any change in their lives. Does this mean that salvation is not real? Certainly not! A great change will come about when you renew your mind. As your mind changes, your life changes. Your mind is the computer. It needs to be re-programed with the word of God.

What you put into the computer is what comes out of it. If you put in garbage, garbage will come out. If you put in the word of God, a life based on the word of God will come out. Many people do not re-program their minds after they are born again. That is why there is no change. Salvation always induces radical changes in a person. The things you used to do, you will do them no more! The things you used to say, you say them no more! The places you used to go, you go there no more! All these great changes will take place because your mind has been freshly re-programed with the word of God.

In the book of Ephesians, Paul describes major changes in people's lives. He describes these changes as "putting on the new man". The new man will steal no more! The new man will put away lying! The new man will put away bad speech! The new man will put away bitterness, wrath, clamour and evil speaking. The new man will now be kind, tender-hearted and forgiving. These great changes have come about because he is renewed in the spirit of his mind. In other words, there is a renewal in the deepest part of the computer. There is a renewal in the spirit of the mind!

That ye put off concerning the former conversation the old man, which is corrupt according to the deceitful lusts; AND BE RENEWED IN THE SPIRIT OF YOUR MIND; And THAT YE PUT ON THE NEW MAN, which after God is created in righteousness and true

holiness. Wherefore putting away lying, speak every man truth with his neighbour: for we are members one of another. Be ye angry, and sin not: let not the sun go down upon your wrath: Neither give place to the devil. Let him that stole steal no more: but rather let him labour, working with his hands the thing which is good, that he may have to give to him that needeth. Let no corrupt communication proceed out of your mouth, but that which is good to the use of edifying, that it may minister grace unto the hearers. And grieve not the Holy Spirit of God, whereby ye are sealed unto the day of redemption. Let all bitterness, and wrath, and anger, and clamour, and evil speaking, be put away from you, with all malice: And be ye kind one to another, tenderhearted, forgiving one another, even as God for Christ's sake hath forgiven you.

Ephesians 4:22-32

PRINCIPLE No. 3

AFTER YOU ARE BORN AGAIN, A GREAT CHANGE WILL COME INTO YOUR LIFE IF YOU LISTEN TO A LOT OF PREACHING

So then faith cometh by hearing, and hearing by the word of God.

Romans 10:17

A great change will come into your life if you listen to a lot of preaching. Anyone who listens to preaching is affected by it. This is because faith comes by hearing. The people who experience a great change are those who become addicted to preaching. After I was born again, I was given preaching tapes of Kenneth Hagin. The greatest upward change in my life came from listening to preaching tapes of Kenneth Hagin.

I once visited a church that I had not been to for eight years. I was amazed by the transformation in the church. They were alive! They were vibrant! They were mature! They were eager! They were flowing! They had grown! They were givers! It was amazing! Then I realized that the church had been listening to the podcast of my preaching. They had been soaking in the word of God and listening to sermon after sermon. Even though I had not seen them for eight years, their transformation was unmistakable.

The best thing you can do for yourself is to make yourself an addict of preaching messages. Faith comes by hearing. You will become a man of faith; a man of great beliefs. Learn how to listen to the same message over and over again. The more you hear the same thing, the more it soaks in deeper. The deeper it soaks into your spirit, the more it produces a change in your life. Perhaps, this is the single most radical life-changing habit I can recommend to you.

Listening to preaching is like going to the university all over again. Universities change people's lives. By the time people qualify from the university, they are changed into lawyers, doctors, engineers, pharmacists, etc. When you listen to preaching, it is like having university lectures at home, in your car, on the move, in bed and in the gym. Expect the most major transformations as you soak in preaching messages!

PRINCIPLE No. 4

AFTER YOU ARE BORN AGAIN, A GREAT CHANGE WILL COME INTO YOUR LIFE IF YOU CHANGE YOUR FRIENDS

Do not be misled: "Bad company corrupts good character."

1 Corinthians 15:33 (NIV)

Another thing that greatly affects your ability to exhibit great change is your friends. Your friends are with you throughout the week. You may spend only two or three hours in church every week but you may spend over thirty hours with your friends in the same week. Obviously, your friends will influence you far more than the church does. The one who spends more time with you influences you more.

It is important for you to change your friends now that you are born again. If you maintain the old friends, I can assure you that you will backslide. When I got born again, I had a whole lot of friends from the world. After I got saved, I realised that it was not going to be possible to maintain these people in my life. Gradually, every single one of them disappeared from my life.

Occasionally, I meet some of these people in town. They are like strangers to me. I do not know where most of my old friends are. My new friends are Christians. I do not have anything to do with the old crowd. After you are born again, there will be no change in your life if there is no change in your friends. Show me your friends, and I will tell you all about your spiritual state!

How can you continue to be friends with the liars, the thieves, the fornicators and the adulterers of this world? How can you be pure if you maintain all these friendships? If you keep your old friends, you will look foolish whenever you try to do what is right. How long can you last, looking odd in the midst of unbelievers?

PRINCIPLE No. 5

AFTER YOU ARE BORN AGAIN, A GREAT CHANGE WILL COME INTO YOUR LIFE IF YOU FELLOWSHIP A LOT

NOT FORSAKING THE ASSEMBLING OF OURSELVES TOGETHER, as the manner of some is; but exhorting one another: and so much the more, as ye see the day approaching.

Hebrews 10: 25

After you are born again, there will be a great change if you fellowship a lot. We are in the world but we are not of the world.

Everything in the world is cold and you are hot. If you take a coal of fire out of the midst of fellow charcoals and set it apart, it will soon grow cold. That is what happens when you are taken out of fellowship. You soon grow cold.

Other church members are your fellow charcoals. As soon as you are lifted out of your fellowship, the meetings and the church, you begin to grow cold.

This is why you must be careful when you travel to a new location. Every new location presents a challenge of fellowship. When you move to a new place, you may fall because you do not get plugged into good fellowship. Every time you travel, you must quickly get into the fellowship. Otherwise, you will fall away and grow cold. In Hebrews, the warning is clear. "Do not forsake the assembling together as is the manner of some." I have seen very strong Christians completely backslide because they stopped going for fellowship.

PRINCIPLE No. 6

AFTER YOU ARE BORN AGAIN, A GREAT CHANGE WILL COME INTO YOUR LIFE WHEN YOU ARE ENDUED WITH THE POWER OF THE HOLY SPIRIT

And, behold, I send the promise of my Father upon you: but tarry ye in the city of Jerusalem, until ye be ENDUED WITH POWER from on high.

Luke 24:49

It takes great power to be a Christian. The world is full of pleasures, temptations and things we desire. The girls desire boys and the boys desire girls! This is normal! It takes the power of God to stop doing what is natural. God knows that we are helplessly drawn to sin. That is why He has given us the Holy Spirit.

You should listen to some of the testimonies of people who are utterly transformed by the power of God. Drug addicts are delivered from drugs! Smokers are able to stop smoking! Fornicators are able to preach to the girls they once slept with!

All these great changes are possible only through the power of the Holy Spirit.

Do you want a great change in your life? Pray and ask for the Holy Spirit. Receive the Holy Spirit and depend on the Holy Spirit! You will be amazed at the great change in your life! Jesus warned the disciples to wait until they were endued with power. Everyone needs to be endued with power. If you are not endued with power you will never see a great change.

PRINCIPLE No. 7

AFTER YOU ARE BORN AGAIN, A GREAT CHANGE WILL COME IN YOUR LIFE IF YOU LEARN HOW TO PRAY AND SPEAK IN TONGUES

For he that speaketh in an unknown tongue speaketh not unto men, but unto God: for no man understandeth him; howbeit in the spirit he speaketh mysteries. But he that prophesieth speaketh unto men to edification, and exhortation, and comfort.

He that speaketh in an unknown tongue edifieth himself; but he that prophesieth edifieth the church. I would that ye all spake with tongues, but rather that ye prophesied: for greater is he that prophesieth than he that speaketh with tongues, except he interpret, that the church may receive edifying.

1 Corinthians 14:2-5

Speaking in tongues builds you up like nothing else. You will not find a shallow unchanged person speaking in tongues for hours. Those who show a great change are those who speak in tongues for hours. As you speak in tongues, your spirit is edified. Your spirit man is built up as you speak in tongues.

When you pray in tongues you call on God in a secret language. You bind demons in the spirit world. Speaking in tongues is a secret weapon given to you by God. Nothing changed my life as much as speaking in tongues. I have learnt to speak in tongues for hours! I prefer to speak in tongues than to pray in English! I pray in the spirit and I pray with understanding! I am charged up like a battery when I speak in tongues. I become like a spiritual powerhouse when I speak in tongues!

The reason why you do not speak in tongues much is because you want to understand yourself. You cannot understand tongues! You have to believe that you are praying to God when you speak in tongues. Speaking in tongues enables you to pray all the time. It enables you to call on God all the time. It is God's gift to us.

You must use the clock to help you pray in tongues. Start at 6.00am and end at 7.00am. Start at 4.00am and end at 5.00am. Start at 3.00pm and end at 4.00pm. Use your clock to tell you how long you have prayed. There is no other way to pray in tongues than to use your clock. When you pray in tongues, you cannot even tell when you have said "Amen". You simply have to learn how to pray by the hour. Speak in tongues and there will be a great change in your life. You will be a mighty powerhouse! All your old problems will fade away and you will enjoy your new life in Christ.

Chapter 4

Seven Great Principles of a Peculiar Life

Who gave himself for us, that he might redeem us from all iniquity, and PURIFY UNTO HIMSELF A PECULIAR PEOPLE, zealous of good works.

Titus 2:14

PRINCIPLE No. 1

AFTER YOU ARE BORN AGAIN, ACCEPT THAT YOU ARE SET APART TO BECOME A PECULIAR PERSON WITH A PECULIAR LIFE

For the grace of God that bringeth salvation hath appeared to all men, Teaching us that, denying ungodliness and worldly lusts, we should live soberly, righteously, and godly, in this present world;

Looking for that blessed hope, and the glorious appearing of the great God and our Saviour Jesus Christ;

Who gave himself for us, that he might redeem us from all iniquity, and PURIFY UNTO HIMSELF A PECULIAR PEOPLE, ZEALOUS OF GOOD WORKS.

Titus 2:11-14

The call of God is a call to be peculiar! To be peculiar means to be markedly different from the usual. Are you happy to be markedly different or do you want to be just like everyone else? To be peculiar means you will deviate from the usual and expected path of life. There are many people who are not happy to be called "a peculiar people."

They just want to be like everybody else. I want to marry like everyone else! I want to have a child like everyone else! I want to dress like everyone else! I want to be rich like everyone else! But it is time to accept that God has called you to exist on a completely different path of life. That is what it means to be born again.

PRINCIPLE No. 2

AFTER YOU ARE BORN AGAIN, YOU ARE SET APART TO BECOME A PECULIAR PERSON WITH A PECULIAR LIFE BY PHYSICAL SEPARATION FROM UNBELIEVERS

Be ye not unequally yoked together with unbelievers: for what fellowship hath righteousness with unrighteousness? and what communion hath light with darkness? And what concord hath Christ with Belial? or what part hath he that believeth with an infidel?

And what agreement hath the temple of God with idols? For ye are the temple of the living God; as God hath said, I will dwell in them, and walk in them; and I will be their God, and they shall be my people.

WHEREFORE COME OUT FROM AMONG THEM, AND BE YE SEPARATE, saith the Lord, and touch not the unclean thing; and I will receive you, And will be a Father unto you, and ye shall be my sons and daughters, saith the Lord Almighty.

2 Corinthians 6:14-18

After you are born again, you will have a peculiar life. You must accept this peculiarity. One of the peculiar things is the peculiarity of being physically separate from unbelievers. Do not fight this. Allow yourself to separate physically from the company of people who do not believe in God the way you do. You will meet them at work and in school.

You cannot really escape from them because you are in this world. But in many ways, you will be separate. Do not company with the world! Do not go out and socialise with unbelievers! Do not go for lunches, dinners and parties with unbelievers. Do not have room mates who are unbelievers. Do not have best friends who are unbelievers. Develop new friends and stay separate in Christ. You cannot have everything. You cannot have your old friends as well as the new friends. You cannot have the old life as well as the new life. You must accept to be physically separate from people who do not believe in the same things that you do.

PRINCIPLE No. 3

AFTER YOU ARE BORN AGAIN, YOU ARE SET APART TO BECOME A PECULIAR PERSON WITH A PECULIAR LIFE BY YOUR PURE AND HOLY LIFESTYLE

And you hath he quickened, who were dead in trespasses and sins; wherein in time past ye walked according to the course of this world, according to the prince of the power of the air, the spirit that now worketh in the children of disobedience:

Among whom also WE ALL HAD OUR CONVERSATION IN TIMES PAST IN THE LUSTS OF OUR FLESH, FULFILLING THE DESIRES OF THE FLESH AND OF THE MIND; and were by nature the children of wrath, even as others.

But God, who is rich in mercy, for his great love wherewith he loved us

Ephesians 2:1-4

Holiness will be the big characteristic that will make you peculiar in this world. The whole world follows the lusts of the flesh and the lusts of the mind. If you are not a believer, you will fulfil the desires of the flesh and the mind. After you are born again, you still have desires in your flesh and desires in your mind. The difference between you and an unbeliever is that you do not fulfil those desires.

The whole world follows its desires for sex. This is why our world has millions of fornicators, adulterers, homosexuals and

42

immoral people. Everyone simply does what he feels like doing. After you are born again, you cannot just do what you feel like doing. That is what it means to born again! Most people in this world are not virgins even though they are not married. Being born again means you will have to live a holy lifestyle. You have to set aside all forms of immorality. That will definitely make you peculiar!

You may have to be a virgin when everyone else is not a virgin! God has called you to be a peculiar person. Do not fight it! Accept it. By accepting to have a holy and peculiar life, you are being delivered from many evils. It is your calling to be peculiar! It is your calling to be a virgin when everyone else is not a virgin!

Look at the verse below. Paul is adamant and strong. He is telling us to not behave as Gentiles. Do not walk as unbelievers walk! Their whole life is a long party of lasciviousness, uncleanness and greediness. You are now a peculiar person! You will live a holy and pure life!

This I say therefore, and testify in the Lord, that ye henceforth walk not as other Gentiles walk, in the vanity of their mind, Having the understanding darkened, being alienated from the life of God through the ignorance that is in them, because of the blindness of their heart: WHO BEING PAST FEELING HAVE GIVEN THEMSELVES OVER UNTO LASCIVIOUSNESS, TO WORK ALL UNCLEANNESS WITH GREEDINESS.

But ye have not so learned Christ; If so be that ye have heard him, and have been taught by him, as the truth is in Jesus: That ye put off concerning the former conversation the old man, which is corrupt according to the deceitful lusts; And be renewed in the spirit of your mind; And that ye put on the new man, which after God is created in righteousness and true holiness.

Ephesians 4:17-24

PRINCIPLE No. 4

AFTER YOU ARE BORN AGAIN, YOU ARE SET APART TO BECOME A PECULIAR PERSON WITH A PECULIAR LIFE BY THE MOTIVATION OF YOUR LIFE

(For after all these things do the Gentiles seek:) for your heavenly Father knoweth that ye have need of all these things. But seek ye first the kingdom of God, and his righteousness; and all these things shall be added unto you. Take therefore no thought for the morrow: for the morrow shall take thought for the things of itself. Sufficient unto the day is the evil thereof.

Matthew 6:32-34

The whole world is running after money. After you are born again, there must be a difference between you and everyone else in the world. One of the differences between you and the world is going to be what motivates you. What motivates the world? The gentiles seek after clothes, food, silver and gold. The peculiar thing about you is going to be that you will not seek after silver, gold, clothes and houses but you will seek after the kingdom of God.

Seek ye first the kingdom of God and His righteousness. These are the words of Jesus. As you seek the kingdom of God, all the things that the Gentiles seek for will be added to you.

The difference between a Christian businessman and a worldly businessman is this: both of them are earning money and both of them are searching for profit. But the Christian businessman is seeking the kingdom of God and His righteousness.

By seeking the kingdom of God and His righteousness, the Christian businessman will make more profit than the secular businessman who is just seeking silver and gold. Seek first the kingdom of God and discover for yourself how God will make a peculiar person prosper.

PRINCIPLE No. 5

AFTER YOU ARE BORN AGAIN, YOU ARE SET APART TO BECOME A PECULIAR PERSON WITH A PECULIAR LIFE BY YOUR KEEPING OF THE SABBATH

a. The Sabbath is a peculiar sign for God's people.

And the Lord spake unto Moses, saying, Speak thou also unto the children of Israel, saying, Verily my sabbaths ye shall keep: FOR IT IS A SIGN BETWEEN ME AND YOU THROUGHOUT YOUR GENERATIONS; that ye may know that I am the Lord that doth sanctify you. Ye shall keep the sabbath therefore; for it is holy unto you: every one that defileth it shall surely be put to death: for whosoever doeth any work therein, that soul shall be cut off from among his people. Six days may work be done; but in the seventh is the sabbath of rest, holy to the Lord: whosoever doeth any work in the sabbath day, he shall surely be put to death. Wherefore the children of Israel shall keep the sabbath, to observe the sabbath throughout their generations, for a perpetual covenant. IT IS A SIGN BETWEEN ME AND THE CHILDREN OF ISRAEL for ever: for in six days the Lord made heaven and earth, and on the seventh day he rested, and was refreshed.

Exodus 31:12-17

Read the scripture carefully. You will see how God notes the Sabbath day. Today, every country marks Independence Day, Empire day, bank holidays, religious holidays and many other such holidays. These holidays show respect for certain events and certain institutions.

After you are born again, you must show your respect for God by honouring the Sabbath day. Unbelievers and non-Christians sleep in their rooms on the Sabbath Day.

By staying home, not going church, not serving God and not listening to the word of God on the Sabbath day, they identify themselves as non-believers. After you are born again, there must be a difference between you and an unbeliever. That difference becomes glaring on the Sabbath day. Today, most Europeans do not go to church on Sunday. It is a sign that they have departed from God. It is a sign that they are non-Christian.

In other parts of the world, most people go to church on Sunday. That is a sign that they have some faith in God. Perhaps there is no greater evidence of your salvation than the change in what you do on the Sabbath day.

b. The Sabbath is a day of rest for God's people.

Also on the tenth day of this seventh month there shall be a day of atonement: it shall be an holy convocation unto you; and ye shall afflict your souls, and offer an offering made by fire unto the Lord. And ye shall do no work in that same day: for it is a day of atonement, to make an atonement for you before the Lord your God.

For whatsoever soul it be that shall not be afflicted in that same day, he shall be cut off from among his people. And whatsoever soul it be that doeth any work in that same day, the same soul will I destroy from among his people.

Ye shall do no manner of work: it shall be a statute for ever throughout your generations in all your dwellings. IT SHALL BE UNTO YOU A SABBATH OF REST, and ye shall afflict your souls: in the ninth day of the month at even, from even unto even, shall ye celebrate your sabbath.

Leviticus 23:27-32

The Sabbath will be a day of rest for you if you follow it. The Sabbath day is a day of rest, whether Saturday, Sunday or Monday. Don't worry about which day of the week it is. There must be a day that you have chosen to set apart for God. A day to rest from secular work!

c. The Sabbath is a day for going to church.

But when they departed from Perga, they came to Antioch in Pisidia, and WENT INTO THE SYNAGOGUE ON THE SABBATH DAY, AND SAT DOWN. And after the reading of the law and the prophets the rulers of the synagogue sent unto them, saying, Ye men and brethren, if ye have any word of exhortation for the people, say on. Then Paul stood up, and beckoning with his hand said, Men of Israel, and ye that fear God, give audience.

Acts 13:14-16

You cannot use the Sabbath for going to the stadium to watch football instead of going to church.   The Sabbath day is the day for going to church! The Sabbath day is a day for serving God and worshipping Him. Jesus went to the synagogue on the Sabbath day. It was His custom to go to church. That was what He did on the Sabbath day. You cannot sleep at home on the Sabbath day. You cannot go to the night club on Saturday night and sleep off on Sunday! You cannot play golf or tennis on the Sabbath day! You cannot do your washing and cleaning on the Sabbath day. You cannot give excuses for not going to church on the Sabbath day. You cannot claim that the Sabbath day is your family time. It is God-time! Your family is not God! You cannot give to your family what belongs to God!

d. The Sabbath is a day for hearing the word of God.

And when the Jews were gone out of the synagogue, the Gentiles besought that THESE WORDS MIGHT BE PREACHED TO THEM THE NEXT SABBATH. Now when the congregation was broken up, many of the Jews and religious proselytes followed Paul and Barnabas: who, speaking to them, persuaded them to continue in the grace of God.

And THE NEXT SABBATH DAY CAME ALMOST THE WHOLE CITY TOGETHER TO HEAR THE WORD OF GOD.

But when the Jews saw the multitudes, they were filled with envy, and spake against those things which were spoken by Paul, contradicting and blaspheming.

Acts 13:42-45

You cannot use the Sabbath day for watching soccer. You must hear the word of God on the Sabbath day. Every born again Christian must hear the word of God on the Sabbath day. God will speak to you on the Sabbath day. You cannot use the Sabbath day for listening to classical music at home! You cannot use the Sabbath day for visiting friends. You cannot use the Sabbath day for listening to the radio. You must listen to the word of God on the Sabbath day. That is what Jesus did!

e. The Sabbath is a day for preaching and teaching the word of God.

And they went into Capernaum; and straightway on the sabbath day he entered into the synagogue, and taught.

Mark 1:21

The Sabbath was a day that Jesus honoured by preaching and teaching the word of God. We need to see you preaching and teaching on the Sabbath day. That is how to be like Jesus. One day you will be just like Jesus; preaching and teaching the word of God on the Sabbath day.

PRINCIPLE No. 6

AFTER YOU ARE BORN AGAIN, YOU ARE SET APART TO BECOME A PECULIAR PERSON WITH YOUR PECULIAR TITHING HABIT

Bring ye all the tithes into the storehouse, that there may be meat in mine house, and prove me now herewith, saith the Lord of hosts, if I will not open you

the windows of heaven, and pour you out a blessing, that there shall not be room enough to receive it.

Malachi 3:10

Tithing is the big difference between the unbelievers and yourself. Tithing makes you peculiar. Unbelievers do not pay anything to God. Unbelievers are wicked and ungrateful to God. They are not grateful for their lives, for their health or for anything God has done for them.

After you are born again you must start paying tithes! It is one of the things that makes you a peculiar person!

Non-Christians do not give anything to God or to His house. It is only those who believe in God who give to Him.

An unbeliever would say, "Who is God? Where is God? What has God done for me? I work very hard and deserve all the money that I earn!" However, when you come to Christ, you know that a man can have nothing except it be given to him from above.

What hast thou that thou didst not receive? Indeed, your tithe is the sign that you believe that all that you have is from God. If you have not paid tithes up till now, please remember that tithing is a sign that you believe in God. After you are born again you must start paying tithes. It is one of the things that make you a peculiar person!

PRINCIPLE No. 7

AFTER YOU ARE BORN AGAIN, YOU ARE SET APART TO BECOME A PECULIAR PERSON WITH DISTINCTIVE BLESSINGS

YE HAVE SAID, IT IS VAIN TO SERVE GOD: and what profit is it that we have kept his ordinance, and that we have walked mournfully before the Lord of hosts?

And now we call the proud happy; yea, they that work wickedness are set up; yea, they that tempt God are even delivered.

Then they that feared the Lord spake often one to another: and the Lord hearkened, and heard it, and a book of remembrance was written before him for them that feared the Lord, and that thought upon his name.

And they shall be mine, saith the Lord of hosts, in that day when I make up my jewels; and I will spare them, as a man spareth his own son that serveth him.

THEN SHALL YE RETURN, AND DISCERN BETWEEN THE RIGHTEOUS AND THE WICKED, BETWEEN HIM THAT SERVETH GOD AND HIM THAT SERVETH HIM NOT.

Malachi 3:14-18

Thank God you are born again. After you are born again, you will experience distinctive blessings. These are blessings that will distinguish you from the world in every way.

The prophecy in Malachi is the prophecy of distinctive blessings. You will experience distinctive blessings because you are born again and are now a servant of God.

As you serve God, there will be a distinction between yourself and those who do not know Him. It is important for you to believe in this fact. You will return and discover that there is a difference between those who serve the Lord and those who do not!

Prosperity is a spiritual thing. You will not prosper unless God wants you to prosper. All the poor and destitute places of this world are unable to rise up in spite of the political decisions that are taken there. Prosperity and well-being are blessings from God. You must decide to walk on with God as a peculiar Christian who enjoys the blessings of God that make you distinct.

Chapter 5

Seven Great Principles of a Supernatural Life

Thou shalt see GREATER THINGS THAN THESE.

John 1:46-50

PRINCIPLE No. 1

AFTER YOU ARE BORN AGAIN, YOU WILL EXPERIENCE THE SUPERNATURAL, THE MIRACULOUS AND THE EXTRA ORDINARY

After you are born again, you must begin to experience signs and wonders. Our God is a God of wonders and supernatural things. When you read the Bible, you cannot escape the presence of signs, wonders and the supernatural. Signs and wonders and supernatural things are promised to the believer. Your life is no longer going to follow a dull, ordinary path.

Why You Should Expect the Supernatural

a. God is a God who does wonders.

Who is like unto thee, O Lord, among the gods? Who is like thee, glorious in holiness, fearful in praises, DOING WONDERS?

Exodus 15:11

b. Jesus told Nathanael that he would see many wonders as he followed Him.

And Nathanael said unto him, can there any good thing come out of Nazareth? Philip saith unto him, Come and see. Jesus saw Nathanael coming to him, and saith of him, Behold an Israelite indeed, in whom is no guile!

Nathanael saith unto him, Whence knowest thou me? Jesus answered and said unto him, before that Philip called thee, when thou wast under the fig tree, I saw thee. Nathanael answered and saith unto him, Rabbi, thou art the Son of God; thou art the King of Israel. Jesus answered and said unto him, Because I said unto thee, I saw thee under the fig tree, believest thou?

THOU SHALT SEE GREATER THINGS THAN THESE.

John 1:46-50

c. Jesus said those born of the spirit would be unpredictable, invisible, and unfathomable just like the wind. Surely, that is supernatural.

The wind bloweth where it listeth, and thou hearest the sound thereof, but canst not tell whence it cometh, and whither it goeth: so is every one that is born of the Spirit.

John 3:8

d. Jesus said signs and wonders would follow believers. Are you a believer? Indeed, you can expect signs and wonders to follow you.

And THESE SIGNS SHALL FOLLOW THEM THAT BELIEVE; In my name shall they cast out devils; they shall speak with new tongues; They shall take up serpents; and if they drink any deadly thing, it shall not hurt them; they shall lay hands on the sick, and they shall recover.

Mark 16:17-18

PRINCIPLE No. 2

AFTER YOU ARE BORN AGAIN, YOU MUST *BELIEVE IN GOD* IN ORDER TO EXPERIENCE A SUPERNATURAL LIFE

Jesus said, Take ye away the stone. Martha, the sister of him that was dead, saith unto him, Lord, by this time he stinketh: for he hath been dead four days.

JESUS SAITH UNTO HER, SAID I NOT UNTO THEE, THAT, IF THOU WOULDEST BELIEVE,

THOU SHOULDEST SEE THE GLORY OF GOD?
Then they took away the stone from the place where
the dead was laid.

And Jesus lifted up his eyes, and said, Father, I thank
thee that thou hast heard me. And I knew that thou
hearest me always: but because of the people which
stand by I said it, that they may believe that thou hast
sent me.

John 11:39-42

If you are to experience a supernatural life, you will have to believe in God. You must believe in the word of God and in the voice of God. It is not possible to experience supernatural things without being a strong believer.

Jesus said to Martha, *"If you believe, you will see the glory of God."* This is an eternal rule. If you believe, you will see the glory of God. I have seen the glory of God in my life because of the things I have believed. I believed in the call of God. I believed God had called me to be a pastor. I believed that I should give myself wholly to the ministry. I believed that I had to abandon all secular activities and focus on the ministry. I believed God would take care of me as I served Him.

All these beliefs led me to the glory of God. I began to see the glory of His provision. I began to see glory of the church developing. I began to see the glory of people being interested in what I was preaching. You will see the glory of God when you believe. If you remain a Doubting Thomas, do not expect to see the glory of God in your lifetime.

PRINCIPLE No. 3

AFTER YOU ARE BORN AGAIN, YOU MUST *BECOME OBEDIENT* IN ORDER TO EXPERIENCE THE SUPERNATURAL

Jesus saith unto her, Woman, what have I to do with thee? mine hour is not yet come. His mother saith unto the servants, WHATSOEVER HE SAITH UNTO YOU, DO IT.

John 2:4-5

In the amazing miracle of turning water into wine, Jesus commanded the servants to pour out the water in the pitchers. It was Mary, His mother, who gave them the master key for bringing on the supernatural. *Whatever He says to you, do it.* If you want to see the supernatural, you must be obedient to the word of God. I have experienced the supernatural by obeying what God said to me. When he spoke to me to write books, I laughed. "Who would want to read my book? I am a nobody living in a corner of Africa." However, I obeyed the Lord and today you are reading this book. Millions of books have been published by obeying the word. The door to the supernatural is obedience!

PRINCIPLE No. 4

AFTER YOU ARE BORN AGAIN, YOU MUST *PRESS YOUR WAY* INTO THE SUPERNATURAL

The law and the prophets were until John: since that time the kingdom of God is preached, and EVERY MAN PRESSETH INTO IT.

Luke 16:16

After you are born again, you must press your way into the things of God. You will not experience the supernatural power of God unless you press hard to enter. The devil is already discouraged and unhappy that you are born again. He is not going to just allow you to experience more victories. He is going to make things difficult for you to progress spiritually. He will fight you every step of your spiritual journey.

Laziness, indifference and laxity will not get you anywhere in the kingdom of God. Make no mistakes about it. The law and the prophets were until John. But now, the kingdom of God has come and everyone must press into it.

All those who sit back and think they will be known because they are honest, sheepish Christians do not understand what is happening. Being happy, honest and sincere is different from pressing hard to enter the kingdom of God and possessing all that belongs to you.

There was a man who was placed by the pool of Bethesda for thirty-eight years. Every time a supernatural miracle was about to occur, another person would press through and enter the water before him.

The impotent man answered him, Sir, I have no man, when the water is troubled, to put me into the pool: but while I am coming, ANOTHER STEPPETH DOWN BEFORE ME. Jesus saith unto him, Rise, take up thy bed, and walk. And immediately the man was made whole, and took up his bed, and walked: and on the same day was the sabbath.

John 5:7-9

I have had to fight to be holy. I have had to press hard to be spiritual! I have had to press my way into the things of God. I have fought to be in full time ministry. I have fought to become a minister of God. I have had to press hard to experience the anointing! I have had to press hard to relate with certain fathers in the ministry. Nothing is given to you on a silver platter! Rise up and press your way into the things of God.

The man by the pool of Bethesda was in the same spot for thirty-eight years. How long do you want to be in the same spot? You have to be active! You have to be aggressive about spiritual things! Do you think that strange woman will just walk away from you? Certainly not! Do you think that wicked man will just stop following you? Certainly not! You will have to fight your way out and press your way into the kingdom of God.

PRINCIPLE No. 5

AFTER YOU ARE BORN AGAIN, YOU MUST BE *LED BY THE SPIRIT* IN ORDER TO EXPERIENCE THE SUPERNATURAL

For as many as are led by the Spirit of God, they are the sons of God. For ye have not received the spirit of bondage again to fear; but ye have received the Spirit of adoption, whereby we cry, Abba, Father.

Romans 8:14-15

Supernatural things begin when you follow the Spirit of God. "As many as are led by the spirit are sons of God." When you were not born again, you were led by your mind and other natural factors. After you are saved, you are no longer led by the philosophies of men and the ideas of the people around you.

Born again Christians are led by the spirit of God! Being led by the spirit of God is what will make the difference in your life. Notice the scripture below. God will set you above your colleagues when you hearken to His voice. The blessing for hearkening to the voice of God is clear. Israel was a nation amongst other nations. God promised that Israel would be greater, better and higher than all the nations around them. What was the condition for this great promise? Hearkening to the voice of the Lord God! Today, listening to the voice of God has that same effect. As you listen to the voice of God, you will be greater, better and higher than all your colleagues.

And it shall come to pass, IF THOU SHALT HEARKEN diligently unto the voice of the Lord thy God, to observe and to do all his commandments which I command thee this day, that THE LORD THY GOD WILL SET THEE ON HIGH above all nations of the earth: And all these blessings shall come on thee, and

overtake thee, if thou shalt hearken unto the voice of the Lord thy God.

Deuteronomy 28:1-2

The prophet Isaiah describes the Lord as the one who leads us in the way we should go. He is the one who teaches us to profit. You will have peace like a river and righteousness like the waves of the sea when you hear and follow the voice of the Lord. Supernatural provision is the hallmark of someone who is led by the Spirit. They thirsted not when He led them through the deserts (Isaiah 48:21). You will not be thirsty when you are led by the Spirit! The desert is a place where you can die quickly of thirst. There is simply no water anywhere. God led the Israelites through this desert and they were never thirsty. You may be going through a desert place. If you follow the Spirit, you will never be thirsty and you will never be hungry.

Perhaps your country is a desert. Perhaps you are in a desert of jobs and prosperity. If you can listen to the Holy Spirit, you will soon be saying, "The Lord is my shepherd, I shall not want." Read this scripture yourself. It is one of the most beautiful prophecies of those who want to be led by the Spirit.

Thus saith the Lord, thy Redeemer, the Holy One of Israel; I am the Lord thy God which teacheth thee to profit, WHICH LEADETH THEE BY THE WAY THAT THOU SHOULDEST GO. O that thou hadst hearkened to my commandments! Then had thy peace been as a river, and thy righteousness as the waves of the sea: Thy seed also had been as the sand, and the offspring of thy bowels like the gravel thereof; his name should not have been cut off nor destroyed from before me. ... And THEY THIRSTED NOT WHEN HE LED THEM THROUGH THE DESERTS: he caused the waters to flow out of the rock for them: he clave the rock also, and the waters gushed out.

Isaiah 48:17-19, 21

PRINCIPLE No. 6

AFTER YOU ARE BORN AGAIN, YOU MUST *DO THE WORK OF GOD* IN ORDER TO EXPERIENCE THE SUPERNATURAL

And he said unto them, Go ye into all the world, and preach the gospel to every creature. He that believeth and is baptized shall be saved; but he that believeth not shall be damned. And these signs shall follow them that believe; In my name shall they cast out devils; they shall speak with new tongues; They shall take up serpents; and if they drink any deadly thing, it shall not hurt them; they shall lay hands on the sick, and they shall recover.

Mark 16:15-18

Miracles, signs and wonders are for those who are going out to do the work of God. "These signs shall follow them that believe." These are the signs that are following those who are going to "all the world" to preach the gospel. Why would God want to do signs, wonders and miracles? God would want to do signs, wonders and miracles because He is helping the commission to be fulfilled. God is not a magician who is seeking an audience. God is not out to do little tricks to impress anyone to earn some dollars. God has a purpose. His purpose is to save the world. He will back anyone who is walking in His purpose. He will help anyone who is going into the world to preach the gospel. He will support the person with signs and wonders.

I left my medical career and launched out into the Great Commission. God has followed this act with many supernatural signs and wonders. God is going to do the same for you as you serve Him and go into "all the world". Expect the miraculous! Expect the supernatural! Expect wonderful things! Expect wonders!

And his disciples asked him, saying, Master, who did sin, this man, or his parents, that he was born blind? Jesus answered, neither hath this man sinned, nor his parents: but THAT THE WORKS OF GOD SHOULD BE MADE MANIFEST in him.

John 9:2-3

Jesus explained why this man was blind. The healing of that blind man was a wonder waiting to happen. God will do wonders just so that the works of God will be manifested.

PRINCIPLE No. 7

AFTER YOU ARE BORN AGAIN, YOU MUST BE JOYFUL AND THANKFUL IN ORDER TO EXPERIENCE THE SUPERNATURAL

Because thou servedst not the Lord thy God WITH JOYFULNESS, and with gladness of heart, for the abundance of all things;

Deuteronomy 28:47

Serving the Lord with joy and gladness opens the door to the supernatural. It is not enough to just serve the Lord. You must serve Him with joyfulness. You must have a good attitude. You must be thankful and sweet-spirited. Do not be mean-spirited, rebellious, grumbling or ungrateful.

When Jesus performed His greatest financial miracle, all He did was to say thanks. Indeed, Jesus is remembered for saying thanks on that momentous day when He fed five thousand people. Long after the miracle had occurred, people referred to the place of the miracle as the place where Jesus had given thanks. Where the miracle occurred was where Jesus had given thanks. Miracles occur when you are thankful. Doors close when you are unthankful, disgruntled and mean-spirited. Doors open when you are grateful, thankful and humble.

And Jesus said, Make the men sit down. Now there was much grass in the place. So the men sat down, in number about five thousand. And Jesus took the loaves; and when he had given thanks, he distributed to the disciples, and the disciples to them that were set down; and likewise of the fishes as much as they would. . .

(Howbeit there came other boats from Tiberias nigh unto the place where they did eat bread, after that the Lord had given thanks:)

John 6:10-11, 23

Be filled with the Spirit by giving thanks and singing with melody in your heart. These are Paul's instructions to the Ephesians. When you are filled with the Spirit, you are filled with the supernatural. Being filled with the supernatural comes by singing and making melody in your heart to the Lord. As you sing and make melody in your heart to the Lord, the spirit of murmuring and grumbling will be taken away from you.

And be not drunk with wine, wherein is excess; but BE FILLED WITH THE SPIRIT; Speaking to yourselves in psalms and hymns and spiritual songs, SINGING AND MAKING MELODY IN YOUR HEART TO THE LORD;

Ephesians 5:18-19

When the Israelites grumbled, evil spirits were drawn to them. They were destroyed by disease, snake bites and other supernatural occurrences. An entire generation was wiped out by their grumbling and murmuring.

Never forget this formula: grumbling, murmuring and complaining bring in evil spirits. Singing, praising God and being thankful bring in the Holy Spirit.

Chapter 6

Seven Great Principles on Spiritual Growth

BUT GROW IN GRACE, and in the knowledge of our Lord and Saviour Jesus Christ. To him be glory both now and for ever. Amen.

2 Peter 3:18

PRINCIPLE No. 1

AFTER YOU ARE BORN AGAIN, ACCEPT THAT YOU ARE EITHER A SPIRITUAL BABY, A SPIRITUAL CHILD OR A SPIRITUAL ADULT

As newborn BABES, desire the sincere milk of the word, that ye may grow thereby:

1 Peter 2:2

That we henceforth be no more CHILDREN, tossed to and fro, and carried about with every wind of doctrine, by the sleight of men, and cunning craftiness, whereby they lie in wait to deceive;

Ephesians 4:14

For every one who partakes only of milk is not accustomed to the word of righteousness for he is AN INFANT. But solid food is for THE MATURE, who because of practice have their senses trained to discern good and evil.

Hebrews 5:13-14 (NASB)

After you are born again, you will have three stages of spiritual growth: the baby stage, the childhood stage and the maturity stage.

Spiritual growth can be likened to growth in the natural. This is true because the Bible clearly describes Christians as spiritual babies, as spiritual children or as spiritually mature people. Today, you must accept that you are one of these three. You are either a spiritual baby, a spiritual child or a spiritually mature person.

PRINCIPLE No. 2

AFTER YOU ARE BORN AGAIN, YOU BECOME A SPIRITUAL BABY AND ARE DOMINATED BY THE FLESH

And you hath he quickened, who were dead in trespasses and sins; Wherein in time past ye walked according to the course of this world, according to the prince of the power of the air, the spirit that now worketh in the children of disobedience: Among whom also we all had our conversation in times past in the lusts of our flesh, FULFILLING THE DESIRES OF THE FLESH AND OF THE MIND; and were by nature the children of wrath, even as others.

Ephesians 2:1-3

After you are born again, you become a spiritual baby who is dominated by the flesh. What are spiritual babies like? Spiritual babies are just like unbelievers who are religious! What is a religious unbeliever? An unbeliever is someone who has not received Jesus as his Saviour. An unbeliever is someone who is not born again. An unbeliever is someone who does not know Christ.

However, there are people who are religious unbelievers. There are some unbelievers who are religious, in that, they go to church, they sing hymns and they pray before they set out on a journey. Such unbelievers, although religious, are actually not born again Christians.

Some time ago, I was religious. I prayed every day. I went to church on Sundays but I did not know Jesus Christ as my Saviour. I was a religious unbeliever.

What are unbelievers like? Unbelievers are described in the scripture above.

An unbeliever is someone who fulfils the desires of his flesh and his mind. He does whatever comes to his mind and follows every natural urge and feeling.

That is exactly how spiritual babies are. They cry and complain all the time. They do not restrain themselves when they have sexual urges and desires. They fulfil every desire they have. Spiritual babies also pray and go to church. In this regard, spiritual babies and religious unbelievers are very similar.

Natural babies also follow every urge that comes to them. They cry anywhere. They eat anywhere. They urinate anywhere. They defecate anywhere at any time. They simply follow all their urges.

There are many people of whom we are not sure whether they are Christians or not. They could either be religious unbelievers or tiny spiritual babies. You must ask yourself today, "Am I a spiritual baby?" If you are born again and you are still fulfilling all your fleshly desires, then you are a tiny little spiritual baby. There is no difference between you and an unbeliever who is equally fulfilling all his fleshly desires.

PRINCIPLE No. 3

WHEN YOU BECOME A SPIRITUAL CHILD YOU ARE DOMINATED SOMETIMES BY THE FLESH AND SOMETIMES BY THE SPIRIT

That we henceforth be no more CHILDREN, TOSSED TO AND FRO, and carried about with every wind of doctrine, by the sleight of men, and cunning craftiness, whereby they lie in wait to deceive; But speaking the truth in love, may grow up into him in all things, which is the head, even Christ:

Ephesians 4:14-15

After you are born again, you may grow into the spiritual childhood stage that is dominated sometimes by the flesh and sometimes by the Spirit resulting in instability and uncertainty.

The main difficulty with a spiritual child is instability. Children run around a lot. They cannot sit still and they have a short attention span. Spiritual children cannot settle down in a church and do not belong to one congregation. Spiritual children are unstable. Every new church and every new prophet who comes on the scene impresses them.

There is no stability in the life of a spiritual child. Children are easily hurt and that is why they cry a lot. Spiritual children are the same. Most people have scars from cuts and bruises they had as children. Spiritual children are easily offended by the pastor or by the ministry. They are easily hurt by someone in church. They leave the church with the slightest provocation.

Are you a spiritual child? Can you be tossed to and fro by every new teaching? Can a prophet prophesy you out of the church you belong to? Some pastors are spiritual children and can be carried away by new ideas. Children can be abducted by strangers, never to be seen again.

One day, a prophet came to one of my pastors who was spiritually mature. He prophesied that he was going to have a new ministry in France and in Francophone countries. He prophesied a new beginning for this pastor. He prophesied that he had been faithful with another man's ministry and God was giving him his own ministry. He virtually prophesied my assistant out of my church.

He said, "It is time to leave where you have been faithful for twenty-five years."

When I heard this story, I asked my pastor how he found that prophetic encounter. His answer was simple. He said, "I had to control myself from bursting out in laughter. I didn't want to offend this prophet by my laughter. I found his prophecy so ridiculous!"

This pastor was too mature to be prophesied out of his position and his God-given place.

Can you be easily prophesied out of your place? Are you easily moved? Are you stable? It is important that you mature out of the spiritual childhood stage and become a mature Christian. Being a spiritual child can be dangerous. Children can be caught by strangers and stolen from their parents.

PRINCIPLE No. 4

WHEN YOU ARE SPIRITUALLY MATURE YOU ARE DOMINATED BY THE SPIRIT

But the FRUIT OF THE SPIRIT is love, joy, peace, longsuffering, gentleness, goodness, faith, meekness, temperance: against such there is no law. And they that are Christ's have crucified the flesh with the affections and lusts. If we live in the Spirit, let us also walk in the Spirit.

Galatians 5:22-25

After you are born again, you may grow into the spiritual maturity stage which is dominated by the spirit resulting in the fruit of the spirit and fruits of righteousness.

When you are spiritually mature, you are dominated by the spirit and not by the flesh. You are dominated by the spirit because the spirit is so big, strong and mature that it dominates the flesh which is now weaker than the spirit. Because your spirit is the stronger and dominant part of you, we see more of the fruit of the spirit.

A mature Christian, therefore, has many fruits of the spirit. "…As the branch cannot bear fruit of itself, except it abide in the vine; no more can ye, except ye abide in me" (John 15: 4).

As you stay in Christ you start to bear fruit. Every tree that stays planted in the ground for some time begins to bear fruit.

As you stay connected to Jesus and are mature in the Lord, you begin to bear much fruit.

Mature Christians have more joy, love, peace and patience. Mature Christians are more gentle and full of goodness. When you come close to a mature Christian, you see meekness and humility. Immature Christians are full of pride and over-confidence. Immature Christians are educated people without true Christian love and patience. Immature Christians lack goodness and kindness. They may speak in tongues but they are immature when they lack goodness, kindness and temperance. There are even pastors who lack maturity. Why would I say so? Some pastors lack patience and Christian love. When a pastor is full of jealousy, bitterness and hatred, it is a sign of immaturity.

PRINCIPLE No. 5

THERE ARE THREE LEVELS OF TEMPTATIONS: TEMPTATIONS OF A BABY, TEMPTATIONS OF A CHILD AND TEMPTATIONS OF THE MATURE

Being forty days tempted of the devil. And in those days he did eat nothing: and when they were ended, he afterward hungered. And the devil said unto him, if thou be the Son of God, command this stone that it be made bread. And Jesus answered him, saying, it is written, that man shall not live by bread alone, but by every word of God.

And the devil, taking him up into an high mountain, shewed unto him all the kingdoms of the world in a moment of time. And the devil said unto him, all this power will I give thee, and the glory of them: for that is delivered unto me; and to whomsoever I will I give it. If thou therefore wilt worship me, all shall be thine.

And Jesus answered and said unto him, get thee behind me, Satan: for it is written, Thou shalt worship the Lord thy God, and him only shalt thou serve.

And he brought him to Jerusalem, and set him on a pinnacle of the temple, and said unto him, If thou be the Son of God, CAST THYSELF DOWN FROM HENCE: For it is written, He shall give his angels charge over thee, to keep thee: And in their hands they shall bear thee up, lest at any time thou dash thy foot against a stone.

And Jesus answering said unto him, it is said, Thou shalt not tempt the Lord thy God. And when the devil had ended all the temptation, he departed from him for a season.

Luke 4:2-13

After you are born again, you may encounter the three types of temptations: the temptations of a baby, which are fleshly temptations, the temptations of a child, which are loyalty and disloyalty temptations, and the temptations of the mature which are temptations of obedience.

Obviously, the temptations of a child are different from the temptations of a grown up. A child may be tempted to steal some sweets whereas a grow-up may be tempted to commit adultery. In the same way, the temptations of a spiritual baby are different from the temptations of a spiritual child or mature Christian.

The temptations of a spiritual "baby" have to do with the flesh. This is because the flesh dominates a spiritual baby. Jesus Christ was tempted in all points just as we are. He experienced temptations of babyhood, temptations of childhood and temptations of maturity. That is how Jesus was tempted in all points. He was tempted with baby points, childhood points and maturity points. He was tempted in all points!

For we have not an high priest which cannot be touched with the feeling of our infirmities; BUT WAS IN ALL POINTS TEMPTED LIKE AS WE ARE, yet without sin.

Hebrews 4:15

The first temptation of Jesus was typical of the temptation of a spiritual baby. Jesus was hungry. His flesh needed food. His flesh was full of desire. Jesus experienced a great temptation when He was asked to turn stone into bread to satisfy His flesh. Babyhood temptations always involve the flesh.

The second temptation of Jesus was typical of a spiritual "child". His loyalties, his convictions and His stability were tested. Satan actually suggested that Jesus change allegiance and worship him instead of worshipping God.

I am sure Jesus almost burst out in laughter. He however quoted the scripture to satan who was daring enough to even suggest that Jesus should change His allegiance. Can you be tempted to leave God? Can you be tempted to leave your church? Can you be tempted to leave your pastor? Can you be tempted to leave your fellowship?

The third temptation of Jesus was typical of the temptation of a mature person. The temptation of the mature has to do with your obedience to God. Jesus was taken to the temple and asked to throw Himself down. Throwing Himself down was intended to provoke God and manipulate the hand of God. But Jesus knew that He must only obey God.

Jesus was not going to be obedient to a devil, even in the smallest matter. When you are a mature Christian your obedience to God is tested even in the smallest matters.

PRINCIPLE No. 6

AFTER YOU ARE BORN AGAIN, YOUR SPIRITUAL AGE DOES NOT CORRESPOND TO YOUR NATURAL AGE

And he came into all the country about Jordan, preaching the baptism of repentance for the remission of sins; ... And the Holy Ghost descended in a bodily shape like a dove upon him, and a voice came from

**heaven, which said, Thou art my beloved Son; in thee
I am well pleased. And JESUS HIMSELF BEGAN TO
BE ABOUT THIRTY YEARS OF AGE, being (as was
supposed) the son of Joseph, ...,**

Luke 3:3, 22-23

After you are born again, you must remember that your
spiritual age does not correspond to your natural age. Being
older in the natural does not mean you are older in the spirit.

Do you think that John the Baptist was spiritually immature
or not? Indeed, I am sure he was mature. Jesus called him the
greatest prophet who ever lived. "For I say unto you, Among
those that are born of women there is not a greater prophet than
John the Baptist: but he that is least in the kingdom of God is
greater than he." (Luke 7:28).

John the Baptist ministered and died around the age of thirty.
Indeed, John the Baptist was a very young man. His spiritual age
did not correspond to his natural age.

Do you think that Jesus Christ was spiritually mature? Of
course He was! But He was only thirty years old when He began
the ministry. Jesus was the most mature spiritual person that ever
walked the earth and yet He only lived to be thirty-three years
old!

Indeed, your spiritual age and your natural age are completely
unrelated. What about the apostles whom Jesus appointed? How
old do you think they were? Most people lead those younger than
themselves. The apostles and disciples were probably younger
than Jesus. Peter, James, John and the others became apostles
when they were young men. Indeed, your spiritual age is not
determined by your natural age. Do not assume that when a
person is older, he is wiser spiritually! Do not believe that you
cannot become great spiritually because you are young. You
can be a great spiritual person even though you are young. The
presence of lustful thoughts does not mean God is not happy with
you. Lustful thoughts are part of a youthful body.

PRINCIPLE No. 7

AFTER YOU ARE BORN AGAIN, YOU MUST GROW UNTIL YOU BECOME A SERVANT OF GOD

Let a man so account of us, as of the ministers of Christ, and stewards of the mysteries of God.

1 Corinthians 4:1

After you are born again, you must graduate from babyhood, childhood and maturity into servanthood.

There are many Christians who have developed through the stages of babyhood, childhood and maturity but have never become servants of God. In my Christian life I have encountered Christians who have love, patience, peace and gentleness. These wonderful qualities are fruits of maturity and results of being dominated by the Spirit. However, many of these people never graduated further to become servants of God.

It is nice for you to be patient, loving, peaceful and gentle. God is calling you to go one step higher and become a servant of God. Today, there are people who introduce themselves to you and say, "I am a lawyer for Christ. I am a doctor for Christ. I am a businessman for Christ. I am a nursing mother for Christ." These people sound pious, peaceful, gentle and loving. They have a sort of holy aura around them and never seem to get into trouble. All that is nice and good! But it is different from becoming a servant of God. When you become a servant of God you have to fight for God's kingdom. When you fight for God's work you may not look and sound so peaceful any longer.

When a man starts to save souls, all sorts of difficulties spring up. Read your history! Learn about the servants of God. Go to the prophets! What a fight Moses had! What a fight Joshua had! What a fight Jeremiah had! Do you think Jeremiah had a peaceful life when he was thrown into prison for God's sake? What about Jesus Christ? What about the apostles, the martyrs, the reformers and the missionaries? Do you think they had it easy? Do you think they floated around in life on a cloud of peace, love, joy, gentleness and goodness? Their lives were more than having these qualities. Fighting is the life of a servant of God! To be a servant of God you may have to contend with earth or hell or both.

You can do more for God than just overcoming your fleshly desires and urges. You can do more for God than being a lawyer for Christ or a doctor for Christ. You can be a servant of God who fights for the souls of men. You can make yourself a saviour of men by fighting the devil who has taken possession of the world and the people that are in it.

Look at the fight men have for money! See how men die in the search for treasures of gold and diamonds under the earth and under muddy rivers.

Look at the fight men have for fame! See how they will sacrifice time, health, friends and life itself to make a name! See how they die for what they believe! Look at the fight that men have for the governments that they prefer! It is time to grow up out of this so-called mature peaceful Christianity and become a servant of God who fights for the souls of men.

Chapter 7

Seven Great Principles of Fruitfulness

Ye have not chosen me, but I have chosen you, and ORDAINED YOU, THAT YE SHOULD GO AND BRING FORTH FRUIT, and that your fruit should remain: that whatsoever ye shall ask of the Father in my name, he may give it you.

John 15:16

PRINCIPLE No. 1

AFTER YOU ARE BORN AGAIN, YOU MUST BECOME FRUITFUL TO SHOW THAT YOU'RE WORTHY OF YOUR SALVATION

For this cause we also, since the day we heard it, do not cease to pray for you, and to desire that ye might be filled with the knowledge of his will in all wisdom and spiritual understanding; that ye might WALK WORTHY OF THE LORD UNTO ALL PLEASING, being fruitful in every good work, and increasing in the knowledge of God;

Colossians 1:9-10

After you are born again, you must show that you're worthy of your salvation by being fruitful.

God expects you to bear fruit to prove that you are worthy of your salvation. Every tree that is planted occupies space and it expected to produce fruit. I planted two mango trees from Guinea in my house. I carried them all the way from Guinea. I paid for their transportation. I protected them from withering and drying up. For many months, I ensured that they were watered. I prevented all those who wanted to discard those seedlings from doing so. As I speak today, those two seedlings are not showing that they are worthy of their salvation. They have produced no fruit. It has been five years of investment and I see no signs that these two trees are worthy of their salvation. I saved them from Guinea and brought them to Ghana and yet there is no sign that they appreciate my great efforts.

Apostle Paul was a blasphemer and injurious to the cause of Christ. God considered that he would be faithful if He saved him. This is the reason why God saved him. God is expecting you to be faithful! He is expecting you to be correspondingly grateful to Him for His great love for you. That is what it means to be fruitful.

According to the glorious gospel of the blessed God, which was committed to my trust. And I THANK CHRIST JESUS OUR LORD, WHO HATH ENABLED ME, for that HE COUNTED ME FAITHFUL, PUTTING ME INTO THE MINISTRY; Who was before a blasphemer, and a persecutor, and injurious: but I obtained mercy, because I did it ignorantly in unbelief. And the grace of our Lord was exceeding abundant with faith and love which is in Christ Jesus.

1 Timothy 1:11-14

PRINCIPLE No. 2

AFTER YOU ARE BORN AGAIN, YOU MUST BECOME FRUITFUL BY BEING PLANTED IN CHRIST

I am the vine, ye are the branches: He that ABIDETH in me, and I in him, the same bringeth forth much fruit: for without me ye can do nothing.

John 15:5

After you're born again, you must press on into fruitfulness by being planted in Christ. It is only when a tree stays in one place that it bears fruit.

After you are born again, you must become fruitful to show that you are abiding in Christ. It is up to you to prove that you are stable and planted in Christ.

After you're born again you must be planted in Christ. The more you are planted, the more fruit you bear! Being planted is what releases you to bear much fruit. Notice how the tree that is planted by the rivers of water bears fruit.

Blessed is the man that walketh not in the counsel of the ungodly, nor standeth in the way of sinners, nor sitteth in the seat of the scornful.

But his delight is in the law of the Lord; and in his law doth he meditate day and night. And HE SHALL BE LIKE A TREE PLANTED BY THE RIVERS OF WATER, THAT BRINGETH FORTH HIS FRUIT in his season; his leaf also shall not wither; and whatsoever he doeth shall prosper.

Psalms 1:1-3

PRINCIPLE No. 3

AFTER YOU ARE BORN AGAIN, YOU MUST BECOME FRUITFUL BY RECEIVING THE HOLY SPIRIT

Upon the land of my people shall come up thorns and briers; yea, upon all the houses of joy in the joyous city: Because the palaces shall be forsaken; the multitude of the city shall be left; the forts and towers shall be for dens for ever, a joy of wild asses, a pasture of flocks; UNTIL THE SPIRIT BE POURED UPON US FROM ON HIGH, AND THE WILDERNESS BE A FRUITFUL FIELD, and the fruitful field be counted for a forest. Then judgment shall dwell in the wilderness, and righteousness remain in the fruitful field.

Isaiah 32:13-16

After you're born again, you must be fruitful because the Holy Spirit is poured out on you.

You may not know the kind of spirit you have! You have received the Holy Spirit. The Holy Spirit is the spirit of God. The Holy Spirit will make you fruitful. Many Christians do not know what they have received. The disciples, James and John, did not know the kind of spirit they had received. They wanted to kill all the people in the village.

And when his disciples James and John saw this, they said, Lord, wilt thou that we command fire to come down from heaven, and consume them, even as Elias did? BUT HE TURNED, AND REBUKED THEM, AND SAID, YE KNOW NOT WHAT MANNER OF SPIRIT YE ARE OF. For the Son of man is not come to destroy men's lives, but to save them. And they went to another village.

Luke 9:54-56

The Holy Spirit is poured out so that we can bear fruit, not to kill people. When the Holy Spirit came on the disciples, they became soul winners. Jesus said they would have power to win the lost when the Holy Spirit came on them. The Holy Spirit is the spirit of fruitfulness. He comes to make you fruitful. He comes to turn you into a soul winner. He comes to bring church growth. If you have the Holy Spirit it is important that you rise up and win souls.

PRINCIPLE No. 4

AFTER YOU ARE BORN AGAIN, YOU MUST BECOME FRUITFUL TO AVOID BEING TAKEN AWAY FROM CHRIST

I am the true vine, and my Father is the husbandman. EVERY BRANCH IN ME THAT BEARETH NOT FRUIT HE TAKETH AWAY: and every branch that beareth fruit, he purgeth it, that it may bring forth more fruit.

John 15:1-2

Do you want to be taken away from Christ? Certainly not! Do you want to fall away? Do you want to be like Judas who at one point knew the Lord but then fell away? Certainly not!

Judas fell away from fruit-bearing activities and began to seek after money.

Those who seek after money do not usually bear much fruit. Getting money and becoming rich is different from being fruitful in Christ. Ministers of God are constantly urging their congregations to become rich and prosper. That is different from preaching the gospel and bearing fruit. Judas veered off into impressive financial schemes aimed at getting him more money and wealth. Today, many Christians have equally veered off into vain jangling and impressive financial schemes. The market place, the businesses and the politics are the desire and focus of many men of God. It is sad to see that many ministers are just like Judas who was focused on getting more money.

Bearing fruit speaks of winning people to Jesus. Bearing fruit speaks of winning souls to God. Bearing fruits speaks of church planting. It is time for you to help the church to grow. It is time for you to do something to show God that you are grateful.

If you do not get into fruit-bearing you will fall away from Christ. You are either moving forward into fruit-bearing or falling backwards into vain jangling.

PRINCIPLE No. 5

AFTER YOU ARE BORN AGAIN, YOU MUST BECOME FRUITFUL TO SHOW THAT YOU ARE NOT BLIND, SHORT-SIGHTED OR FORGETFUL

For if these things be in you, and abound, they make you that ye shall neither be barren nor unfruitful in the knowledge of our Lord Jesus Christ. But he that lacketh these things is BLIND, and CANNOT SEE AFAR OFF, and hath FORGOTTEN that he was purged from his old sins.

2 Peter 1:8-9

Three serious diseases afflict born again Christians. Shortsightedness, blindness and forgetfulness!

After you are born again, you must avoid being diagnosed as short-sighted, blind, and forgetful.

People who are not fruitful are often short-sighted. They cannot see beyond their small family and their small city. They have not opened their eyes to see afar off.

There are many countries in this world. There are many places that need Jesus. People need the Lord! The church is filled with short-sighted men and women who do not care about what is happening behind their walls. Is that what you want to be like? Read the scripture above. Those who are barren cannot see afar off. Are you afflicted with spiritual short-sightedness?

People who are not fruitful have forgotten many things. They have forgotten that eternity is approaching. People who are not fruitful have forgotten that people do not get saved by osmosis. Unfruitful people have forgotten how someone made great efforts to get them saved. They have forgotten how people prayed for them to be converted. They have forgotten how much money was spent by others to get them saved. I hope you are not suffering from spiritual forgetfulness.

People who are not fruitful are often blind. Unfruitful people cannot see eternity. Unfruitful people cannot see heaven! They cannot see hell! They are detached from all these spiritual realities! That is why they do nothing for God. Beware of blindness! Do not just focus on our temporary world! You must have another world in view!

After you are born again, you need to be fruitful otherwise you will be diagnosed as being short-sighted, forgetful or blind.

PRINCIPLE No. 6

AFTER YOU ARE BORN AGAIN, YOU MUST BECOME FRUITFUL BECAUSE THAT IS WHY GOD IS PROTECTING YOU

Now will I sing to my wellbeloved a song of my beloved touching his vineyard. My wellbeloved hath a vineyard in a very fruitful hill:

And he fenced it, and gathered out the stones thereof, and planted it with the choicest vine, and built a tower in the midst of it, and also made a winepress therein: and he looked that it should bring forth grapes, and it brought forth wild grapes.

And now, O inhabitants of Jerusalem, and men of Judah, judge, I pray you, betwixt me and my vineyard.

What could have been done more to my vineyard, that I have not done in it? Wherefore, when I looked that it should bring forth grapes, brought it forth wild grapes?

And now go to; I will tell you what I will do to my vineyard: I will take away the hedge thereof, and it shall be eaten up; and break down the wall thereof, and it shall be trodden down:

And I will lay it waste: it shall not be pruned, nor digged; but there shall come up briers and thorns: I will also command the clouds that they rain no rain upon it.

Isaiah 5:1-6

After you are born again, God will protect you so that you can bear much fruit. This beautiful prophecy in Isaiah is for all of us. It shows us that God does not protect His vineyard for nothing. You are His vineyard. He is protecting you because He is expecting you to bear fruit.

When you go to church, you are being watered and nurtured. Why is that? What does God want from you? Does He want your money? Does He want your house? Does He want your car? I do not think so! All the silver and the gold in this world belong to God. God wants fruits! God wants your gratefulness! He wants your love! He wants souls! Fruitfulness is whatever you will do that will bring more souls to the Lord.

God wants fruits from you! Do you want Him to keep on protecting you? Do you want Him to keep on loving you? I believe you do! It is time to rise up and become fruitful in the

Lord. God will send angels to keep you in your ways so that you can bear fruits onto eternity. Expect divine protection as you bear divine fruits!

PRINCIPLE No. 7

AFTER YOU ARE BORN AGAIN, YOU MUST BECOME FRUITFUL BECAUSE THAT IS YOUR DESTINY

And God blessed them, and God said unto them, be fruitful, and multiply, and replenish the earth, and subdue it: and have dominion over the fish of the sea, and over the fowl of the air, and over every living thing that moveth upon the earth.

Genesis 1:28

After you're born again, you must press on into fruitfulness because that is your destiny. All children of Adam are blessed with the gift of being fruitful and multiplying.

After you are born again, you must press on into the blessing of being fruitful! When God created man He blessed him with the blessing of fruitfulness. Receive that blessing and walk in it!

You are blessed with the blessing of multiplying yourself. This is the first blessing of mankind. To be fruitful in Christ is to multiply yourself in Christ. Bring somebody who is just like you to the Lord. Lead others to Jesus Christ! Bring people to church! Visit somebody at home! Follow up a lost backslider! Call those who have stopped coming to church. Help someone to be established in church! That is what it means to be fruitful.

Chapter 8

Seven Great Principles of Establishment

But the God of all grace, who hath called us unto his eternal glory by Christ Jesus, after that ye have suffered a while, make you perfect, stablish, strengthen, settle you.

1 Peter 5:10

E

stablishment means to make something stable!

Establishment means you have become permanent!

Establishment means you are settled in a position!

Establishment means you are accepted and recognized!

Establishment means to gain control of something!

God establishes people! He makes them permanent, stable and settled. That is exactly what He wants to do to you in Christ. There are wonderful examples of people that God established. He can establish you in whatever role He has placed you. He can establish you in Christ. God established Samuel as a prophet. He also established David as a king. Today, He is in the business of establishing you as a Christian.

Don't you want to be a stable and permanent Christian? Don't you want everyone to accept and recognize you as a believer? Don't you want to gain control of your spiritual life so that you can grow in the Lord? See how the Lord established His servants Samuel and David. He will do it for you!

1.   **Samuel was established as a prophet. From that time there was no question that Samuel was a prophet.**

And Samuel grew, and the Lord was with him, and did let none of his words fall to the ground. And all Israel from Dan even to Beer-sheba knew that SAMUEL WAS ESTABLISHED TO BE A PROPHET OF THE LORD. And the Lord appeared again in Shiloh: for the Lord revealed himself to Samuel in Shiloh by the word of the Lord.

1 Samuel 3:19-21

2.   **David was established as a king over Israel.**

And Hiram king of Tyre sent messengers to David, and cedar trees, and carpenters, and masons: and they built

David an house. And DAVID PERCEIVED THAT THE LORD HAD ESTABLISHED HIM KING OVER ISRAEL, and that he had exalted his kingdom for his people Israel's sake. And David took him more concubines and wives out of Jerusalem, after he was come from Hebron: and there were yet sons and daughters born to David.

2 Samuel 5:11-13

3. **David's children were established as the future leaders of Israel.**

And when thy days be fulfilled, and thou shalt sleep with thy fathers, I will set up thy seed after thee, which shall proceed out of thy bowels, and I WILL ESTABLISH HIS KINGDOM. He shall build an house for my name, and I will stablish the throne of his kingdom for ever. I will be his father, and he shall be my son. If he commit iniquity, I will chasten him with the rod of men, and with the stripes of the children of men: But my mercy shall not depart away from him, as I took it from Saul, whom I put away before thee. And thine house and thy kingdom shall be established for ever before thee: thy throne shall be established for ever.

2 Samuel 7:12-16

4. **God has established the earth.** The earth is an established planet. This is why the planet is stable in its seasons and cycles. We all know what to expect on this amazingly stable planet that rotates about the sun along with the other planets.

The earth is the Lord's, and the fulness thereof; the world, and they that dwell therein. For he hath founded it upon the seas, and ESTABLISHED IT UPON THE FLOODS.

Psalms 24:1-2

Seven Great Principles about Establishment

PRINCIPLE No. 1

AFTER YOU ARE BORN AGAIN YOU MUST BECOME ESTABLISHED IN THE FAITH

And so were the churches ESTABLISHED IN THE FAITH, and increased in number daily.

Acts 16:5

Wherefore I will not be negligent to put you always in remembrance of these things, though ye know them, and be ESTABLISHED IN THE PRESENT TRUTH. Yea, I think it meet, as long as I am in this tabernacle, to stir you up by putting you in remembrance;

2 Peter 1:12-13

Wherefore when we could no longer forbear, we thought it good to be left at Athens alone; And sent Timotheus, our brother, and minister of God, and our fellowlabourer in the gospel of Christ, TO ESTABLISH YOU, and to comfort you concerning your faith:

1 Thessalonians 3:1-2

As you can see, becoming established in Christ was very important to the apostles. They always wanted those whom they had led to Christ to be established in God. Peter wanted to stir up Christians until they were established. Paul was sending Timothy and other ministers to help establish the believers at Thessalonica. This book is being sent into your hands to help you to be established in Christ.

PRINCIPLE No. 2

AFTER YOU ARE BORN AGAIN YOU WILL BECOME ESTABLISHED BY TELLING THE TRUTH AND BEING HONEST

The lip of truth shall be established for ever: but a lying tongue is but for a moment.

Proverbs 12:19

Telling the truth and being honest with yourself is the master key to spiritual growth. The Bible teaches us that by speaking the truth we may grow up in Christ Jesus.

"But speaking the truth in love, may grow up into him in all things, which is the head, even Christ" (Ephesians 4:15). Being honest about your struggles and about realities in Christ will help you to overcome the devil. Most Christians are not honest about their challenges. People like to present a perfect picture but things are not perfect for anyone. Most Christians think that the Christian sitting next to them in church cannot have any problems, especially the ones that they are having. This hypocrisy makes Christians fall away because they feel they are not worthy to be among the saints. Be open! Be honest about your challenges and you will receive help. If you say you have a hearing problem, someone will give you a hearing aid. If you say you have no hearing problem, no one will give you a hearing aid. If you say you have a spiritual problem someone will give you some spiritual aid. If we walk in the light as He is in the light, we will have true fellowship. (1 John 1:7).

PRINCIPLE No. 3

AFTER YOU ARE BORN AGAIN YOU BECOME ESTABLISHED BY PUTTING AWAY WICKEDNESS FROM YOUR LIFE

A man shall not be established by wickedness: but the root of the righteous shall not be moved.

Proverbs 12:3

After you are born again you become established by putting away wickedness from your life. Establishment comes by removing the wicked from your company and your presence.

When you are born again, you have transitioned from a life of wickedness into a new life in Christ. Old things are passed away and all things are become new (2 Corinthians 5:17). It is essential that you put away the wickedness of your past life and embrace the new things that God is bringing into your life.

PRINCIPLE No. 4

AFTER YOU ARE BORN AGAIN YOU BECOME ESTABLISHED BY LISTENING TO THOSE WHO HAVE BEEN CHRISTIANS BEFORE YOU

For I long to see you, that I may impart unto you some spiritual gift, to the end ye may be established;

Romans 1:11

Every purpose is established by counsel: and with good advice make war.

Proverbs 20:18

Without counsel purposes are disappointed: but in the multitude of counsellors they are established.

Proverbs 15:22

After you are born again you become established by listening to and receiving from those who have been Christians before you.

You cannot make it in Christ without the input of older Christians. Those who have been in Christ longer than you will know more about dodging evil and surviving as a Christian. They have been tested in the same temptations that you are now experiencing. Establishment comes by listening to good advice from older Christians, pastors and teachers. If you do not listen to the pastor's teaching and to his words of advice, you will be destroyed before you can be established in Christ.

PRINCIPLE No. 5

AFTER YOU ARE BORN AGAIN YOU BECOME ESTABLISHED BY TAKING GOOD DECISIONS

The king by judgment establisheth the land: but he that receiveth gifts overthroweth it.

Proverbs 29:4

After you are born again you need to take good decisions that help your Christian life. The scripture above says that the king by judgment (wise decisions) establishes the land. Without practical decisions you will fall back into all your old ways. You need to separate yourself practically from all that is evil in your life. You need to take back your keys which are with the enemy. Do not let him have the keys to your house! Do not let him walk in at any time! Many Christians simply fall out of Christ because they do not take practical decisions that will help them. The things I used to do, I do them no more! Do not go to the places you used to go to before. Do not have the friends that you used to have before. Do not maintain the old relationships that you used to have. Take wise decisions and you will distance yourself from the devil and all that he seeks to destroy you with.

PRINCIPLE No. 6

AFTER YOU ARE BORN AGAIN, YOU BECOME ESTABLISHED BY VALUING YOUR SALVATION

When any one heareth the word of the kingdom, and UNDERSTANDETH IT NOT, then cometh the wicked one, and catcheth away that which was sown in his heart. This is he which received seed by the way side.

Matthew 13:19

After you are born again, you are in great danger of falling away because you lack the understanding of the principles of salvation.

Our salvation is not as simple as it sounds. Christianity is quite a complex religion. Christianity involves complicated topics like the shedding of the blood of Jesus, the cross of Christ, the reality of heaven and hell and the amazing love of God. These concepts are not so easy to understand. Indeed, even the sin of man and the wretchedness of the state of humankind is not so easy to comprehend. You need to study and understand the deep principles that have given rise to the wonderful salvation that we are experiencing.

Salvation is not as simple as filling a form of membership. Your membership to a church does not mean your membership in Christ. The devil is looking for Christians who do not understand what has happened to them.

As you can see in the scripture above, the wicked one is ready to come and steal the word of God from those who do not understand what has happened to them. It is time to go deeper if you want to be established. You must understand more than you do today. Salvation is more than raising your hands for prayer! Salvation is more than being prayed for! Salvation is more than coming forward during a church service!

Salvation is the act of being rescued from the power of darkness and being transferred into the kingdom of God by the supernatural blood of Jesus Christ. This wonderful salvation takes place because of the amazing love and forgiveness of God. Indeed, there is much more to understand if you want to protect yourself from being struck out by the wicked one. Demons know far more than you can imagine. They can see deep into your heart and know that you do not really understand what salvation is. It is time to get a deeper understanding of what you are into since you came to know Christ.

PRINCIPLE No. 7

AFTER YOU ARE BORN AGAIN, YOU BECOME ESTABLISHED IN CHRIST BY UNDERSTANDING THE PRINCIPLES IN THE WORD OF GOD

But he that received seed into the good ground is he that heareth the word, and UNDERSTANDETH IT; which also beareth fruit, and BRINGETH FORTH, some an hundredfold, some sixty, some thirty.

Matthew 13:23

The Lord by wisdom hath founded the earth; by understanding hath he established the heavens.

Proverbs 3:19

Through wisdom is an house builded; and by understanding it is established:

Proverbs 24:3

Understanding can be defined as knowing "principles". A principle is a basic truth that guides your actions. It is an explanation of the fundamental reasons why things are the way they are. When you know the principles of Christ you understand what is happening and why it is happening.

In this book of Seven Great Principles, you will understand what salvation is and why you are experiencing what you are experiencing. By having a deeper understanding of Christianity you will be able to go higher and do more in Christ.

In medical science, having an understanding of how the heart works has enabled human beings to actually transplant hearts from one person to another. It has enabled human beings to take the heart of a dead person and make it work again. These medical miracles are the result of a deep understanding of how the body works. As your read this book you will receive more principles of how Christianity works and what you must to do to enjoy your Christian life. You will bear much fruit because your understanding is deeper and stronger through these principles. Indeed, a deep understanding is the basis of bearing much fruit.